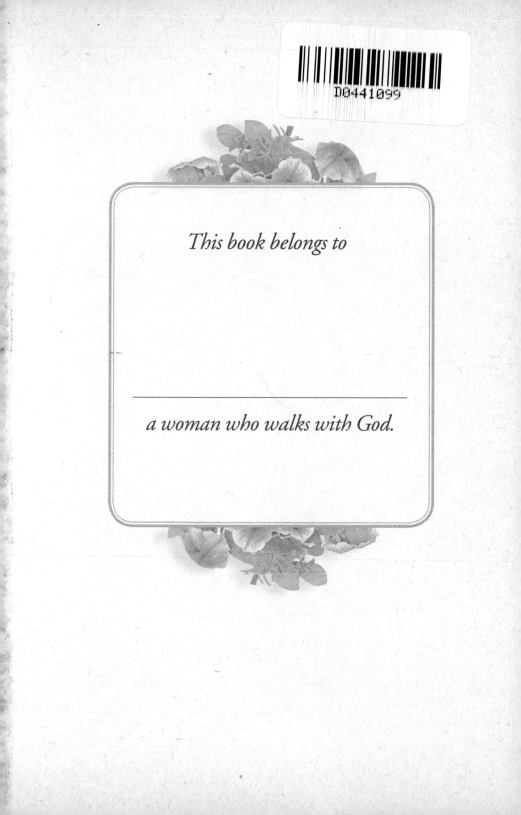

This book belongs to

_____

a woman who walks with God.

A WOMAN'S WALK WITH GOD

ELIZABETH GEORGE

HARVEST HOUSE PUBLISHERS
EUGENE, OREGON

Cover design by Dugan Design Group, Minneapolis, Minnesota

Cover photos © Dugan Design Group; iStockphoto/wwing

A WOMAN'S WALK WITH GOD
Copyright © 2000 by Harvest House Publishers
Eugene, Oregon 97402
www.harvesthousepublishers.com

Library of Congress Cataloging-in-Publication Data
    George, Elizabeth, 1944–
    [God's garden of grace]
    A woman's walk with God / Elizabeth George
        p. cm.
    Originally published: God's garden of grace. Eugene, Or.: Harvest House Publishers, ©1996.
    Includes bibliographical references.
    ISBN 978-0-7369-5091-6 (pbk.)
    ISBN 978-0-7369-5092-3 (eBook)
    1. Christian women—Religious life. I. Title
    BV4527.G459 2000
    248.8'43—dc21   99-059248

Printed in the United States of America

15 16 17 18 19 20 21 22 / BP-CD / 12 11 10 9 8 7 6 5 4

For my parents Henry and Ruth White
whose home has always been a rich garden of virtues.

Contents

1

Preparing for Greater Growth

~

Several years ago when I spoke at a women's retreat in Bellingham, Washington, I stayed overnight in the home of a warm and gracious couple. After parking the car in the garage behind their house, we walked through their backyard garden and right past an exquisite apple tree. Being from Southern California where all we know is orange trees, I commented on how beautiful the tree was. With that, my hostess Jennifer began telling me the story of their apple tree.

Since moving into their home, Jennifer's husband, Tom, has tended this magnificent tree. Wanting to enjoy its Golden Russet apples, Tom has worked hard to improve the tree's production. After doing some research, he even grafted on some branches from their older Gravenstein apple tree as well as several new shoots from a Spartan apple tree. Through the years, Tom has nurtured, fertilized, watered, pruned, trained, sprayed, and protected this tree, and his efforts have paid off as he's seen the tree improve over time.

And that tree's yield is quite incredible. Tom has to prop up the branches to keep them from breaking when they're loaded with apples! Then, when the fruit is ripe, it's Jennifer's turn. She takes the tree's three kinds of apples and cooks, cans, mashes, sauces, dries, stews, slices, dices, and freezes them. Anything you can do with apples, she does! In fact, for dessert the evening I was there, Jennifer served apple crisp, and when I left the next morning she handed me a plastic bag full of dried apples to eat on the plane.

As I think of this couple's apple tree, I can't help but wonder about the fruit of our lives as Christian women. Should you and I as women of God pay any less attention to our own fruitfulness, in our case the spiritual kind, than Jennifer and Tom do to their apple tree? Shouldn't we be actively cultivating the fruit of the Spirit in our lives in order to reflect the glory of God and the beauty of Christ? But what exactly can you and I do to grow these spiritual fruit? What practical steps can we take toward becoming more like Christ as we walk alongside Him day by day?

Understanding the Fruit of the Spirit

Well, my friend, just as Tom studied to learn more about his apple tree and the fruit it bears, you and I need to study God's Word so we can better understand the fruit of the Holy Spirit and how it grows. Throughout the Bible, the word "fruit" refers to evidence of what is within. If what's inside a person is good, then the fruit of that person's life will be good. But if what's inside is rotten, the fruit of that person's life will be bad. Any person who has received Jesus as Savior and Lord and has Christ living within will bear good fruit—the "fruit of righteousness" (Philippians 1:11)—as God shines forth in his or her life.

The fruit of the Spirit has been described as "those gracious habits which the Holy Spirit produces in the Christian."[1] In Galatians 5:22-23, the apostle Paul lists these "gracious habits": "The fruit of the Spirit is love, joy, peace, patience, kindness, goodness, faithfulness, gentleness, [and] self-control." I'm sure that, like me, you've undoubtedly longed for these noble traits to be characteristic of your life—but how can we make that happen? *Perhaps if I just try harder...* we may find ourselves thinking. But Jesus teaches and models that such individual, do-it-yourself effort isn't the answer. Instead, it's exciting (and comforting!) to realize that the fruit of the Spirit can be produced in our lives in the same way that it was produced in Jesus' life! We will enjoy a harvest of spirituality when we yield to God and allow His Spirit to work in us as we walk through life.

As you and I walk together through God's list of the fruit He deserves in our life, we'll look not only at their beauty and bounty but also at each individual fruit. But we must never forget that all nine fruit stand together: love, joy, peace, patience, kindness, goodness, faithfulness, gentleness, and self-control make up our walk with God. They are like a string of Christmas lights—there is one string with many lights that, when plugged into the electrical socket, all light up at once. However, if one bulb goes out, the entire string goes out. That's how God's fruit is borne in our lives. No one of them can be missing, and all must be evident to be God's fruit.

We also need to remember that because these fruit act as one, they are each borne in our lives in the same way. They are like a watch, which contains many parts. A watch can be taken apart for cleaning and repair, but each piece must be in place for the watch to run. In this book, you and I will carefully take apart each fruit of the Spirit, and then we'll see how they all work together to present a whole.

And as a whole, these characteristics are all produced in the same way. Everything that is said of one characteristic is true of the other eight. They are one and the same fruit, interwoven and related to one another, produced as we look to God.

Walking by the Spirit and cultivating the fruit of the Spirit is what this book is all about. You and I can enjoy a closer walk with God and bear much fruit as we surrender our lives to Him. As we examine each fruit of the Spirit, we'll also be looking at Jesus' life to see its expression in His life. As we follow the real-life example of God's Son, and walk in obedience, we will indeed bear fruit that glorifies our Creator and Lord.

Understanding the Problems

Before we begin learning about our walk with God, we would do well to acknowledge a couple of "stumbling stones" we'll encounter along the path. First, legalism is a problem for us Christians today just as it was for believers in Paul's day. Legalism is the careful keeping of a set of rules which exceeds what is written in Scripture (1 Corinthians 4:6). In fact, Paul wrote to the Galatians because some false teachers (called Judaizers) were teaching that, despite their faith in Christ, they must follow the Old Testament laws. This teaching ran counter to all that Jesus taught and to the fundamental truth that people come to God by faith alone. It also fostered an ugly form of legalism and religion based strictly on works. So Paul called believers to allow the Spirit of God to fulfill the Law for and through them. If they would only "walk by the Spirit" (Galatians 5:16,25), they would be abiding by the Law in a natural and beautiful way.

Another problem you and I have in common with Galatian believers, dear friend, is one we'll face until the day we die, and that is the conflict between the flesh and the Spirit which begins the instant we put our faith in Jesus Christ. Paul writes, "For the flesh sets its desire against the Spirit, and the Spirit against the flesh; for these are in opposition to one another, so that you may not do the things that you please" (Galatians 5:17). These fleshly pursuits result in "deeds of the flesh" (5:19), sins and vices which Paul lists in Galatians 5:19-21—"immorality, impurity, sensuality, idolatry, sorcery, enmities, strife, jealousy, outbursts of anger, disputes, dissensions, factions, envying, drunkenness, carousing, and things like these."

Which weaknesses are evident in your life, beloved? Ask God to help you recognize your fleshly tendencies and deeds by praying David's heartfelt words: "Search me, O God, and know my heart; try me and know my thoughts; and see if there be any wicked way in me" (Psalm 139:2324 kjv). Then confess anything God reveals to you and submit once again to the transforming power of His Spirit. That's what walking by the Spirit is all about!

Understanding the Call to "Walk by the Spirit"

Aren't you glad that right after the ugly list of sins, Paul moves on to the fruit of the Spirit (Galatians 5:22)? In sharp contrast to the deeds of the flesh, Paul paints a lovely picture of the fruit produced in our lives as we walk by the Spirit. When you and I walk by the Spirit we "will not carry out the desire of the flesh" (5:16) and we can have victory over the flesh. But how exactly do we as Christians walk by the Spirit?

In simple terms, walking by the Spirit means living each moment in submission to God. Walking by the Spirit means seeking to please Him with the thoughts we choose to think, the words we choose to say, and the actions we choose to take. And walking by the Spirit means letting Him guide us each step of the way. It's letting Him work within us so that we can bring glory to God.

Understanding "Abiding in Christ"

Although I'll be giving you many practical suggestions for cultivating the fruit of the Spirit in our lives as we journey through this book, we must never lose sight of the fact that the Bible clearly teaches, "There is none who does good, there is not even one" (Romans 3:12). Paul himself lamented, "For I know that nothing good dwells in me, that is, in my flesh" (Romans 7:18). It is only as we walk by His Spirit that we show forth Christ in our lives. And God gives us the grace to do this as we abide in Christ.

Do you ever wonder what "abiding in Christ" means? In the eloquent allegory of John 15, Jesus says, "I am the true vine" and calls His disciples—then and now—to "abide in Me" (verse 4). Only by abiding in Him can Jesus' followers bear fruit (verses 2,4-5). This call comes as Jesus shares His final words of instruction with His small flock—words concerning His death, words of comfort and warning, words of peace and prayer. He explains that, although He will be gone, they will still have fellowship with Him if they "abide" in Him. The same opportunity exists for you and me today, my friend. To bear fruit for God's kingdom, we must abide in Christ. Such "abiding" has been defined as "continued fellowship with the Lord,"[2] "dwelling in His fellowship and being submissive to His will,"[3] and keeping "contact with Jesus… a constant contact."[4]

I'm sure you join me in wanting to abide in Christ! But what can we *do* to keep our contact with Jesus constant? What can we *do* to abide in our Lord—to remain close to God and dwell in Him as He dwells in us? What can you and I *do* to share more of His life and experience more fully His presence in our lives? Consider these practical steps for enjoying a closer walk with Him.

Spending time in God's Word is one step we can (and should!) take daily to abide in Christ. Dr. Everett F. Harrison writes, "Abiding cannot be maintained apart from giving the words of Christ a regnant [reigning] position in the heart (cf. Colossians 3:16). He is honored when His Word is honored."[5] So we must be diligent about spending time in God's Word. Do we read, study, and meditate on a regular basis? Frequently enough? Daily? Is our time in God's Word rich and meaningful, or are we merely going through the motions? Because God's Word reveals "the thoughts of his heart to all generations" (Psalm 33:11b KJV), we are able to have sweet communion with Him when we read the Scripture. Besides, there is really no other way to know His thoughts, His ways, or His heart. Oh, pray for God to give you an insatiable appetite for rich fellowship with Him through His Word, an appetite that nothing else can satisfy!

Spending time in prayer is another act of worship that makes it possible for you and me to commune with and abide in Christ. Dr. Harrison points out that Christ "honors His Word when the saints come pleading its promises in prayer,"[6] and a saint of old states simply, "A prayerless life means a life without Christ, without faith, without work, without consistency."[7] As yet another believer has observed, "No blessing of the Christian life becomes continually possessed unless we are men and women of regular, daily, unhurried, secret lingerings in prayer."[8]

Well, dear friend, would an outside observer describe you or me as a person of "regular, daily, unhurried, secret lingerings in prayer"? Is prayer a vital link between us and God—who is our solace and our strength? Do we seek to know more about God, His heart, and His purposes through the holy communion of prayer? If you and I are to abide in Christ and be women who walk with God, we must do all we can to enhance our prayer life.

Obeying God's commands also enhances our abiding in Christ. Therefore, our waking prayer each morning should be to make choices that honor Him and His Word. In John 15:10, Jesus teaches that such obedience was an essential part of His own constant communion with the Father: "If you keep My commandments, you will abide in My love, just as *I* have kept my Father's commandments, and abide in His love" (emphasis added). In keeping His Father's commandments Jesus stayed close to His Father, modeling for us obedience to our heavenly Father.

It's a paradox, beloved. It is *as* we walk by the Spirit—abiding in Christ and obeying God's commands—that the *Holy Spirit* produces *His* fruit in our life. Theologian John F. MacArthur comments on this paradox in the Christian life: "Although we are commanded to exhibit spiritual fruit, it can never be produced except by yielding to the Holy Spirit."[9] You see, the fruit that results in our life *because* of our obedience is evidence of the *Spirit* at work *in* us. We can do nothing strictly on our own to bring about that fruit. But as God's will increasingly becomes our highest aim, our tarnished lives are transformed by the Holy Spirit into a glittering trophy of grace which points the world to Him.

Renewing our commitment to Christ seems appropriate here as we prepare for greater growth. Before anything—or anyone—can grow, it must be alive. Therefore you and I need to ask ourselves a simple question: Am I alive spiritually?

In the Book of Romans, we read that "all have sinned" (3:23); that "the wages of sin is death" (6:23); and that "God demonstrates His own love toward us, in that while we were yet sinners, Christ died for us" (5:8). Jesus took on our sin, dear one, and died in our place. Have you accepted that wondrous truth and named Jesus *your* Savior and the Lord of *your* life? As the Bible instructs us, "If you confess with your mouth Jesus as Lord, and believe in your heart that God raised Him from the dead, you shall be saved" (Romans 10:9). Before you can experience any spiritual growth, this seed of faith in Jesus must take root in your heart and life.

So are you alive? Only three answers are possible— "yes," "no," and "I'm not sure." If you answered "no"—if you have not accepted Jesus as Lord and Savior—you can set foot on the path of walking with God and growing in Him right now by earnestly praying these words:

> Jesus, I know I am a sinner, but I want to repent of my sins and turn and follow You. I believe that You died for my sins and rose again victorious over the power of sin and death, and I want to accept You as my personal Savior. Come into my life, Lord Jesus, and help me obey You from this day forward.

If you aren't sure if the seed of faith has taken root in your heart, you may want to say a prayer of *re*commitment. You could pray these words:

> Jesus, I know that in the past I asked You into my life. I thought at that time that I was Your child, but my life hasn't shown the fruit of my belief. As I again hear Your call, I want to make a real commitment to You as the Lord and Master of my life.

Or perhaps the following prayer better fits your circumstances:

> Dear Lord Jesus, I know that in the past I asked You into my life. I want to be Your child, I think and hope that I am Your child, but I want to know that I am Your child. Lord, give me the reassurance that I have eternal life through You because of Your death on the cross for my sin (1 John 5:13).

Beloved, if you're not sure where you stand with God, let Him know right now in a very personal prayer. After all, God loves you, and He already knows your heart, and He wants to be in close fellowship with you.

Finally, if you answered—or can now answer—"Yes! I know I am alive in Christ now and forever!" take a few moments to thank God and praise Him for all that Jesus has done for you. Commit yourself anew to walking the path of greater growth in God's grace. The following lyrics may help you worship:

You paid much too high a price for me;
Your tears, your blood, the pain;
To have my soul just stirred at times,
Yet, never truly changed.
You deserve a fiery love that won't ignore your
    sacrifice,
Because you paid much too high a price.[10]

It's the prayer of my heart—for myself and for you—that God would use this book to prompt us to grow in God's grace so that we are "truly changed." May we be moved to give ourselves wholly to Christ. And may we seek nothing other than to follow Him and to exhibit the radiance of the Savior in us as we walk with God. After all, "the world has yet to see what God can do with and for and through and in a man [or woman] who is fully and wholly consecrated to Him."[11]

ATTITUDES
of the
Fruit of the Spirit

2

Looking to God for Love

❧

The fruit of the Spirit is love.

GALATIANS 5:22

On June 11, 1994, our younger daughter Courtney was married to Paul Seitz in a lovely ceremony at our home church. As I sat on the front pew, the mother-of-the-bride for the first time, I was awed by the sights and sounds that filled the chapel. They were the product of a whirlwind of busyness on the part of the bride and groom's families and friends. The bouquets of off-white rosebuds and ivy had been arranged by one of Courtney's college friends, and a friend of the family was taking pictures. My fellow choir members were helping with the music—a prelude of hymns on the organ, chimes at precisely two o'clock, and a trumpet to herald Courtney's entrance. Long-time friends had decorated the front platform with green foliage, white blossoms, and trailing ivy from their garden at home. The setting was picture perfect!

One of the greatest pleasures for me that day was having so many family members at the wedding. On the George side of the aisle were my three brothers and their wives, my parents, and my mother-in-law. On the other side of the aisle were Paul's mother and a sister-in-law. Paul stood at the front of the church with his father, two brothers, and brother-in-law. I thanked God for the blessing of a caring family who wanted to share this special event with Courtney and Paul.

All day long I had felt like a cast member in a school play. I had a role to play and I busily went about my duties—until my older daughter Katherine walked down the aisle. She was the last of the bridesmaids, her sister's maid of honor. Suddenly the wedding and its accompanying emotions became very real!

Then I heard the trumpet announce Courtney's arrival. I rose and turned to see standing at the back of the church my wonderful husband Jim with a radiant and confident Courtney on his arm. The moment we'd all been planning for so long was here. Jim's eyes were moist as he escorted his daughter, and Courtney was strong and regal in the classic gown Paul's mother had lovingly made. As the two of them slowly marched down the aisle, I thought about the fact that a whole new life lay before Paul and Courtney.

Now it was time for the ceremony itself, the moment of eternal significance for which all the busyness served only as a humble prelude. As an ordained minister, Jim officiated the wedding and presided over their vows as no one else could have. With the authority of a minister and the love of a father, he summoned the young couple to make a sober commitment, before God and all the people gathered, to love one another for the rest of their days. As I sat sniffling, I heard Jim call upon Courtney and her new husband to love one another with Christ's love.

Yes, I thought, that's what God intends this wedding and all of life to be about—Christian love. His design calls for a bride and groom who love to become a husband and wife who love and, in turn, parents and grandparents who love. He wants His love reflected in brothers and sisters who love, uncles and aunts who love, families who love, and friends who love. I again thanked God for the many evidences of His love that were before my eyes and filling my life that special day.

Learning About Love

We can't read very far in the New Testament without realizing that love is important to God. He calls us as women who love God...

- to walk in love (Ephesians 5:2)

- to love one another (John 15:12)

- to love our husbands and our children (Titus 2:4)

- to love our neighbor (Matthew 22:39)

- to love our enemies (Luke 6:27)

Scripture also teaches that "God *is* love" (1 John 4:8, emphasis added) and that His Son Jesus Christ loved us and "gave Himself up for us [as] an offering" (Ephesians 5:2). We also see love's supremacy when Paul places it first on his list of the fruit of the Spirit (Galatians 5:22).

As children of God, you and I, dear one, are commanded to show forth the kind of love we see modeled by our heavenly Father and His Son. Jesus says very clearly, "This is My commandment, that you love one another; just as I have loved you" (John 15:12). And exactly how has Jesus loved us? And what does the kind of love we're supposed to extend to people look like? We find answers to these questions when we turn to God and His Word. After all, God is love and God is the source of all love, so it makes sense to look to the Scriptures to learn what *He* says about love! Let's look now at five basic principles from God's Word that can help us to understand Christian love.

Principle #1: Love is an act of the will. Every fruit of the Spirit requires decisions, and love is no different. It's hard to love under difficult circumstances, yet that's exactly where most of life is lived, isn't it? I don't know about you, but I especially need love when I'm tired, when I'm suffering in some way, when I'm hurting, or when I'm feeling burdened down. At difficult times like these, I usually don't feel up to loving other people. That's when—I'm learning—it's necessary to activate the will if I am to follow through with actions of love. Commentator William Barclay points out that love "is…a feeling of the mind as much as of the heart; it concerns the will as much as the emotions. It describes the deliberate effort—which we can make only with the help of God…."[1] Christian love, you see, is an act of the will which "needs to be directly cultivated."[2]

Yes, the kind of love Christ modeled calls for deliberate decisions and a conscious effort. His love *in* us is what enables us to give that love when we want to withhold; to reach out to others when we are tired and want to rest; to serve when we want to be served; and to help others when we ourselves are hurting. No wonder Dr. George Sweeting wrote, "Love is work. It demands both conscious and unconscious effort. It demands a continuous, twenty-four-hour-a-day commitment."[3] This kind of love, of course, comes only from God, which is why you and I so desperately need His grace to give it!

For a better understanding of love consider the acts of the will behind the love of God and Jesus revealed in the Bible:

- God so loved the world, that He *gave* His only begotten Son (John 3:16, emphasis added);

- The Son of Man did not come to be served, but *to serve,* and *to give* His life (Matthew 20:28, emphasis added);

- Jesus "*resolutely* set His face to go to Jerusalem" (Luke 9:51, emphasis added) where He would die for us.

Giving, serving, heading for Jerusalem, dying on a cross—these acts of love are acts of the will, not gestures prompted and powered by mere emotion. It is God who gives us the will to love and the ability to act according to our decisions to love in the ways He calls us to love. Will you look to Him to fill you with the kind of love that gave, served, and died to self, the kind of love modeled by our Savior? This, dear one, is one way we walk with God!

Principle #2: Love is action—not just words. Love is also something we *do,* not merely the words that we *say.* Yet acting on our love is not always easy—as a wife knows who pulls into the driveway at 5:30 p.m. followed closely by her husband! Both of them have put in a long day at the office, so... *who* is going to fix the meal, wash the dishes, and do the laundry? Love means that, even when you and I are exhausted and just want to sit down and do nothing, we cook, serve, and wash. You see, love has work to do, and love does that work—love takes action—even when doing so requires strenuous effort. Our actions—backing up our words—are the proof of our love. That is why we are called to love not with word or with tongue only, but "in deed and truth" (1 John 3:18). I'm sure that Courtney is continuing to discover what the *words* of her marriage vows mean as she daily lives them out through *works* of love performed, with God's help, for Paul. I'm also sure that she's learning she has to look to God to enable her to extend to her husband (and all the other people in her life) this kind of serving love.

And now, my dear friend, where has God placed *you* to show

forth love by your actions? Using a phrase from author, wife, mother, homemaker, and grandmother Edith Schaeffer, to whom can *you* demonstrate love "in the day-by-day, mundane circumstances of life"?[4] Every family member provides you with an opportunity to put on the work clothes of love and to serve. If you go daily to a job, love has work to do there as well. If you live with roommates, roll up your sleeves and challenge yourself to do the work of love. In your neighborhood, your volunteer activities, your church, your places of recreation, you are to show forth God's love not only by words and attitudes but by your actions. And God's Spirit, at work in *you*, will cause the glorious fruit of love to blossom in your life as you walk with Him and do His work of love.

Principle #3: Love reaches out to the unlovely. Don't you find it easy to love gracious individuals, mature Christians, and people who say, "Thank you!" when you do something nice? Yes, it's easy to love the lovely, but it's much harder to love the unlovely! I know that people who are cruel, hateful, or unappreciative present a tremendous challenge for me when it comes to loving them.

Yet this is exactly what Jesus calls us to do as women who love Him. In the Sermon on the Mount, He shocked His listeners by saying, "You have heard that it was said, 'You shall love your neighbor, and hate your enemy.' But I say to you, love your enemies, and pray for those who persecute you in order that you may be sons of your Father who is in heaven; for He causes His sun to rise on the evil and the good, and sends rain on the righteous and the unrighteous" (Matthew 5:43-45). Jesus then reminded His hearers that anyone—even those who do not believe in God or follow Christ—can love the lovely: "If you love those who love you," Jesus continued, "what reward have you? Do not even the tax-gatherers do the same? And if you greet your brothers only, what do you do more than others? Do not even the Gentiles do the same?" (verses 46-47). In a parallel account in the Gospel of Luke, Jesus said, "If you love those who love you, what credit is that to you? For even sinners love those who love them. And if you do good to those who do good to you, what credit is that to you? For even sinners do the same" (6:32-33).

Do you see that God's kind of love calls us to love the unlovely just as He Himself does when, for instance, He loves each one of us? God's love is never deserved—it simply *is*. And that's the kind of love you and I are to extend to one another, enemy as well as friend, the unlovely as well as the lovely. Thank God that when the Spirit is at work in our lives, He enables us to do what Jesus commands us to do: "Love your enemies and do good…and you will be sons of the Most High; for He Himself is kind to ungrateful and evil men" (Luke 6:35).

Who in your world falls into the "unlovely" category? Who is irritating, bothersome, ungrateful, or even evil and unrighteous? Who is it that makes your life difficult and brings you misery and heartache? Each one of these people is to be the object of your love. After all, as author Jerry Bridges points out, "To recognize that there is someone I do not love is to say to God, 'I do not love You enough to love that person.'"[5] Through His Spirit, God provides the grace we need to extend His love to the needy people we encounter. Through His Spirit, God enables us to love just as He loves—everyone…all the time…and without conditions.

Principle #4: We need God to help us love. Just as you and I need God's help for each of the fruits of the Spirit, we rely on God for love. In the Sermon on the Mount, Jesus observed that it is quite natural to love those who love us, but it transcends the laws of nature to love those who hate us. Left only to our natural ways, we would hate our enemies. But Christ calls us to love our enemies by allowing God to love them through us when we can't do it on our own.

William Barclay writes, "[Love] means that no matter what a man may do to us by way of insult or injury or humiliation we will never seek anything else but his highest good...never...seek anything but the best even for those who seek the worst for us."[6] Clearly, we need God to help us love those who hate us! And, when we walk with God and love the unlovely with His love, we become a testimony to what He can do in a person's life. Our life then bears the mark of God because only He can enable us to serve the very person who insults, snubs, or hurts us. In fact, such injury makes us far more dependent on God as we seek to obey His command and love the unlovely.

I recently read about Bishop Whipple of Minnesota, a missionary known as "The Apostle to the Indians." In talking about his life work, he said that for thirty years he simply tried to see the face of Christ in the faces of the Indians he ministered to—to love them for Christ's sake.[7] Do you seek to love the difficult, ungrateful, unkind, unlovely people in your world for Christ's sake? If you can see Jesus in the person who causes you pain, you will— by the power of the Holy Spirit—be able to extend God's love to that person (Romans 5:5). God's love is there for us to give, and we who follow Christ need to remember that those who are hardest to love are the ones who need it most.

Principle #5: Love expects nothing in return. Isn't it true that when we are nice to someone, we expect that person to be nice to us? And when we are loving toward someone, we expect that same kind of treatment in return? But when Jesus calls us to love our enemies and do good to them, He tells us to do good to them "expecting nothing in return" (Luke 6:35). When we love as God loves and, like Him, are "kind to ungrateful and evil men" (Luke 6:35), we find we need to love without any thought of personal reward.

And, as a question wives often ask me reveals, we may find

that ungrateful person in our own home! "Liz," I hear, "I've been serving my husband, but he isn't doing anything in return. I'm doing all I can to show him that I love him, but I feel totally unappreciated and even taken advantage of. Should I stop making an effort to serve him?" Maybe you've had similar feelings. What *does* a wife do in a situation like this?

Even—if not especially!—in our own home, we need God's Spirit to be at work in us if we are to truly love as Christ would have us love. It helps both of us to remember that God is kind to ungrateful men (Luke 6:35). And don't forget—this is the kind of love God offers to us in Jesus (Romans 5:8,10)! So, when you and I serve our husbands (or anyone else), we are to serve simply because God lives in us and wants to extend His love to all people through us (Romans 5:5).

And here's another thought from God's Word to help us: We are to love and serve as if the person before us were Jesus Himself! In John 13:34, Jesus Himself says, "A new commandment I give to you, that you love one another, even as I have loved you." And isn't that what Ephesians 5:22 means—"Wives, be subject to your own husbands, as to the Lord"? The Amplified Bible reads, "Wives, be subject...to your own husbands as [a service] to the Lord."[8] In the same passage, husbands are also called to love their wives "just as Christ also loved the church and gave Himself up for her" (verse 25). You see, the love the Bible tells us to extend in our marriage, our home, our neighborhood, our church, and the world at large is *not* self-seeking. Instead, it expects nothing personal in return. Its only intent is to love as Jesus loved while praying for others to respond to God's message of love through us.

Defining Love

As these five principles of biblical love clearly reveal, love is *the sacrifice of self.* This simple definition seems to crystalize all that the Bible teaches about love.

Dr. John MacArthur elaborates: "Love is not an emotion. It is an act of self-sacrifice. It is not necessarily feeling loving toward a particular person. It may not have any emotion connected with it (Romans 5:8). God always defines biblical love in terms of self-sacrifice."[9] It's obvious that since love is the sacrifice of self, it involves effort, not merely emotion. It demands action, not just feelings. It is something we do, not something we only feel or say.

I well remember learning as a young mother that love is sacrifice. Katherine, our first baby, was every mother's dream. She was smiling and responsive. She loved people and she loved being held. Since she was so easy to care for and so much fun to be with, we took her everywhere we went. But Courtney, our second baby, had colic from day one! For the first six months of her little life, she screamed and writhed in pain. Red-faced and uncomfortable, she was completely unresponsive to any acts of love on our part. Some days it wasn't easy to live under the same roof with her!

Courtney was indeed a challenge for me. Yet I kept caring for her, loving her, doing all the acts a loving mother could do—feeding her, holding her, rocking her, and bathing her as she fought and screamed. And not only were our days long, but so were our nights. Sleep came for Courtney—and therefore for us—only as a result of her being exhausted. I certainly didn't *feel* love for her, but—by the grace of God—I *gave* love. It was a time for me to offer the sacrifice of self, to choose to do the works of love and extend love to a not-so-lovely-to-be-with baby without getting anything positive in return. Then, one wonderful day, Courtney relaxed and smiled, and she has been a sweetheart ever since! With the end of colic and Courtney's change of behavior, I continued to love her in a mother's sacrificial way as I had before, but, I have to admit, the sacrifice was then much more rewarding!

And you, dear one? How are you doing when it comes to

loving sacrificially? When you and I go before the Lord in prayer, He will help us and show us where we tend to be selfish and where He'd like us to love more sacrificially. He will remind us that we are to obey God as we walk with Him and love one another... even when we don't feel like doing so! And He will help us recognize opportunities to move beyond speaking words of love to doing the actual work of love. As we look to God's Spirit to empower us to give this kind of sacrificial love, may we pray along with St. Francis of Assisi, "O Divine Master, grant that I may not so much seek to be loved...as to love."

Living Out Love

It helps me as a Christian woman who loves God and yearns for a closer walk with Him to see my call to live out love as an assignment from God to love anyone and everyone He chooses to place in my path. Maybe this story about something I do at my house every day will help you to live out love.

Beside my front door at home I've planted some impatiens. This means that the first thing I see every morning when I open my door to go for my walk are these sad, drooping, thirsty flowers slumped over on the porch. In fact, I have to be careful when I open the door or I'll step on them and crush them!

Now I've been trying to grow impatiens for a long time. I've planted them every year with no success—until these few plants, which were leftovers stuck randomly into the ground at the last minute several years ago. Yet they are the only impatiens that have ever made it. Because of where they are—by the doorstep—they don't receive any water from the sprinklers. So every day I must get my watering bucket, go over to the faucet, fill up the bucket, and carry water to these poor little flowers. After all, if they don't get water, they'll die.

Some days I enjoy this little chore and delight in watering my impatiens. On other days, however, I feel irritated: "Why can't you grow and thrive like my other flowers do?" Or, resenting them and the extra effort they demand, I want to yank them up and toss them into the trash can—especially on those mornings when the green barrel is out by the curb and very convenient! In my tiredness, I don't want to take the extra time or put forth the extra energy to water them. I'd rather give up on them and just let them die. On my rebellious, selfish days, I say, "I don't need this! My life would be easier without these flowers!"

But through the years I've kept up my "bucket brigade." I know that if I don't fill my bucket at the faucet and give my impatiens life-giving water, they will die. So I water them every morning before I go on my walk. The only other time I step out my front door is to get the mail in the afternoon. And, miracle of miracles, as I open the door, these perky, pretty impatiens are smiling up at me! As I look down at them, I'm glad I watered them. No, I didn't necessarily *feel* like doing it, but I did it anyway: I acted on my will, not my feelings. I made the decision and put forth the effort to give the flowers water and keep them alive.

Tending to impatiens has shown me (and I hope you, too!) one way you and I can view the challenge of loving the people God places in our path. We may not necessarily *feel* like loving them, but when you and I allow God to fill us up with *His* life-giving love, we can then carry *His* love to others and pour it out into their lives. The love is not ours—it's God's. But when we present our empty selves to the *Source* of love and are filled by *Him,* then we are able to share *His* love with thirsty people. When we act on our will instead of our feelings, make the decision to love, and put forth the effort to love, God is able to pass on *His* love to others through us.

And if, for example, I am to love my husband the way I want to love him, I need to be filled by God's love every day. I must choose to go to God and present my empty self to Him. Then when He fills me with His love, I am then able to go back to Jim and pour out God's love on Jim. My bucket brigade goes on all day long, for Katherine and Courtney too, and for anyone else God allows to cross my path.

And I confess—I have my hard days! But on the hard days, when I frequently run dry, I go back to God many times so that He can fill me again and again with His love for the people I encounter. When, for instance, I offer a friendly greeting to a woman who doesn't respond, my flesh says, "Well, if that's what I get for being nice, forget it!" But I know that is exactly when I need to run to God and have Him fill me afresh with His love for that woman so I can share it with her. She is someone God wants to show His love to, and I can let Him do so through me. I can let myself be the vessel that carries His love to her.

At times, the love God fills me with in the morning seems bountiful and unlimited, and I can share His love until the sun goes down. But then come those days—those *hard* days!—when I seem to be beating a path back to God minute after minute. Maybe the task is harder, maybe the heart of the person I'm trying to love is harder, maybe my own heart is harder, or maybe I'm not spending enough time with Him to receive what I need to share—I don't know. I do know, though, that only as I keep turning to God can I keep loving the people He places in my path.

Once again, it's God's love, but I'm the empty vessel. It's His "water" that fills me…if I let Him. And, unlike me with my bucket for the impatiens, God *always* wants to fill me. *And* He will do so as many times as I need Him to in the course of a day… and throughout my life. After all, He is the One "who gives to all men generously and without reproach" (James 1:5). He is limitless love, and He is willing and patient as He fills us with His love to share with others. Then, between the two of us, God and I can get the job of loving done!

I hope and pray that this illustration from my daily life helps you, too, dear one, to look to God for His love...and then to live out that love.

Love Lived Out by Ruth

I love looking to the Bible for examples of women who walked with God. And I think that in Ruth we have an example of sacrificial love in the many ways she lived out God's love for a hard-to-love woman, her mother-in-law, Naomi.

Ten years before the story begins, Naomi had moved to Moab from Bethlehem with her husband and two sons. The Bible says, she "went out full" (Ruth 1:21). Then, while they lived in Moab, her sons married and Naomi's family grew to include two daughters-in-law, Orpah and Ruth. But, as Naomi explained to her friends when she returned to Bethlehem after the death of her husband and two sons, "the Lord has brought me back empty" (1:21). Orpah had chosen to stay in Moab, so Naomi returned to Bethlehem alone, except for Ruth. As people welcomed her, she said to them, "Do not call me Naomi [which means "pleasant"]; call me Mara [which means "bitter"]" (verse 20).

Now living in Bethlehem with Naomi, Ruth had the opportunity to live out God's love for her mother-in-law. She rolled up the sleeves of her robe and went to work loving this hurting, dried-up, bitter woman. During harvest season, she served Naomi by gleaning in the barley fields (2:23). Ruth provided for her mother-in-law and herself through the backbreaking labor of the "barley brigade." Every morning as the sun rose, Ruth went out into the fields to glean the barley that had been left uncut by the reapers for the poor and needy. (As widows, she and Naomi certainly qualified!) But merely gathering the grain didn't make it useful. So, after carrying the grain in the skirts of her robe all day long, a tired Ruth then had to beat the barley with a stick to separate the grain from the chaff until it was usable (2:17). Morning after morning, until the harvest was over, Ruth rose early before daybreak to get barley from the fields; and evening after evening she returned after dark to Naomi with a basket of grain and, figuratively speaking, a bucket of love. Ruth sacrificed herself and allowed God to provide for Naomi through her.

Beloved, is it possible that you know a Mara—someone God has put in your life (and perhaps even in your own family) who feels "empty" but who is actually filled with bitterness, heartache, and pain? Loving that person will mean turning to God each day, looking to Him to be your source of love, and going to Him—perhaps quite often!—for a fresh filling of His love. Loving that person will require the sacrifice of self.

Love Lived Out in You

One way we walk in love—God's love—is to look to Him to fill us with His love…the kind of love that we've been learning is an act of the will, that takes action rather than being content with mere words, that extends itself to the unlovely, that gives for the sake of loving, and that involves the sacrifice of self. Most important of all, you and I need God to help us love, and I have an assignment for you which will demonstrate God's ability to help you love the way He wants you to love: Pick the person God has placed in your life who is most difficult to love and put these principles of love into action. Then watch what happens in your heart *and* in the life of that person!

As you consider this assignment and all that you've read about in this chapter, be sure and spend some time praying to the God of love. Confess to Him all your unlovely thoughts about this unlovely person, any attitudes toward him or her that are contrary to God's loving ways, and any past failures to love him or her through your actions or your words. Ask God to enable you to follow His Son's commands to "love your enemies, do good to those who hate you, bless those who curse you, pray for those who mistreat you" (Luke 6:27-28). As we've learned, God wants to do that for you. You just need to open yourself up to receive from Him His endless supply of life-giving, life-changing love.

Things to Do Today to Walk in Love

1. Begin loving the people God puts in your path by first loving those people at home. As the saying goes, "What you are at home is what you are!" So *be* a woman who walks in God's love…at home.

2. Go to God throughout the day for a fresh supply of His love to share. At the first hint of waning love, look to the Lord of love.

3. Remember that your assignment is to serve (Galatians 5:13).

4. Remember Jesus, who "did not come to be served, but to *serve,* and to *give* His life a ransom for many" (Matthew 20:28, emphasis added).

3

Offering the Sacrifice of Joy

⁂

The fruit of the Spirit is...joy.
GALATIANS 5:22

One year on a beautiful autumn Sunday, Jim and I drove to a church in central California so that he could conduct an ordination service for one of his former students from The Masters Seminary. At lunch after the morning ceremony, we learned that we were only 45 minutes away from Sequoia National Park. So, when lunch was over and we were back in the car, Jim suggested that we drive through the park to see the fall leaves.

Well, off we went! Driving to and through the park, we enjoyed the spectacular colors and God's striking handiwork. However, as the shadows lengthened in the afternoon and the temperature dropped, we began to look for a place to warm ourselves with some hot coffee. Eventually we found the one lodge that hadn't yet closed for the winter. After parking the car, Jim and I walked along the trail toward the rustic stone building. As we crossed over a little bridge, we stopped and looked at the brook that flowed beneath it and sounded so pleasant and refreshing. Peering over the rail, we were surprised to discover the cause of the water's sweet sound. We saw piles of large, jagged rocks that were impeding the water's surface, even redirecting its path. Nevertheless, the little brook gave forth utterly joyful sounds! Both Jim and I marveled that something so traumatic could cause something so lovely!

Yet isn't this stream a picture of what real life is like—or at least of what the Christian life should be like? Our lives are filled with disappointments, crises, tragedies, heartaches, affliction, and struggles—just as Jesus said (John 16:33)! But the good news is, that as you and I encounter disquieting rocks that impede *our* progress, disturb *our* tranquility, break the surface, and redirect *our* path, God can give us the joy we need to produce sounds of praise to Him.

Beloved, Jesus desired that our joy might be full (John 16:24), but affliction, loss, stress, and pain can too easily rob us of any sense of joy. But, when we turn our gaze upon God in the midst of our suffering, we suddenly find the power we need to praise Him despite the pain and to give thanks for His goodness…even when things are not so good. Thanks to the working of His Spirit in us, you and I can experience joy that transcends circumstances and transforms something traumatic into something truly lovely.

What the Bible Says About Joy

For a number of years at a Bible institute I had the privilege of taking a class of women through the Book of Philippians, Paul's sparkling little epistle of joy. When I first prepared my lectures for the course, I was struck by the Bible's many references to joy, the next grace on Paul's list of the fruit of the Spirit. What do we learn about joy from the Bible, especially from the more than 70 New Testament references to joy?

First, we see that *joy is important to Jesus.* At the Passover meal He shared with His disciples shortly before His crucifixion, Jesus described the special relationship He would have with His disciples if they would abide in Him and His love. He closed this section of His teaching by saying, "These things I have spoken to you, that My *joy* may be in you, and that your *joy* may be made full" (John 15:11, emphasis added). Jesus wanted His disciples to know the joy of fellowship with Him, joy to the fullest!

Next, we see that genuine *joy*—which is rooted in Christ— *is an expression of godliness.* You see, joy is a sure sign of the presence of God in our lives. Put differently, our joy is "the joy of God passing through a Christian,"[1] "a joy whose foundation is God."[2] Although joy is basic to godliness, it often seems to be missing from our lives despite the fact that, as children of God, we have some great reasons to be joyful.

Reason #1—Our joy is permanent. Because our joy is rooted in our all-loving and unchanging God, our joy is permanent. In John 16:22 Jesus says that "no one takes your joy away from you." However, one thing that can rob us of the joy God provides is our failure to walk by the Spirit (Galatians 5:16). The Holy Spirit causes this fruit to grow in our lives *as* we abide in Christ and walk in obedience to His ways.

Reason #2—Our joy is always available. Since it is rooted in our faithful and ever-present God, our joy is always available. That's why you and I can "rejoice in the Lord always" (Philippians 4:4)! Whatever the circumstances of our life, we have ready access to the Source of true joy anytime we turn to Him.

Reason #3—Our joy is also inexpressible (1 Peter 1:8). Joy in the Spirit is "joy beyond speech."[3] Described as "a foretaste of the joy of heaven,"[4] Christian joy cannot be fully expressed or articulated.[5] We can't explain why we experience joy when nothing in our life suggests we should be joyful.

I hope you understand now why we must acknowledge that true spiritual joy is *not* happiness. "Happiness" is a state of good fortune and prosperity related to and dependent on our circumstances. If all is going well, we are happy; but as soon as some dark cloud or irritation enters our life, our happiness vanishes. Happiness can be a false joy and, since easy circumstances are not life's norm (John 16:33), happiness is elusive. In fact, the apostle Paul preached the truth that "all who desire to live godly in Christ Jesus will be persecuted" (2 Timothy 3:12). God's joy is a gift of grace to us as we encounter the hardship and tribulation and persecution of life in this world, and this supernatural joy, given through God's Spirit, transcends all conditions of life.

As God's children through the new birth, you and I are able to drink deeply from God's unending stream of joy—regardless of what life offers us! Pause now and praise God that our joy as Christians...

- Is not dependent on circumstances, but on the spiritual realities of God's goodness, His unconditional love for us, and His ultimate victory over sin and darkness.

- Is not based on our efforts, accomplishments, or willpower, but rather on the truth about our relationship with the Father through the Son.

- Is not merely an emotion, but the result of choosing to look beyond what appears to be true in our life to what is true about our life in Christ.

In summary, our spiritual joy is not "an experience that comes from favorable circumstances [but] is a sense of well-being that abides in the heart of the person who knows *all is well between himself and the Lord* (emphasis added).[6]

The Sources of Joy

Well, dear child of God, just as we take our empty self to God to be filled with His love, we also go to Him—the Source of true joy—when we feel empty of Christian joy. And, for five reasons, we can receive that joy inexpressible from Him.

First of all, as the psalmist knew, *God Himself* is a primary source of our joy. The psalmist reveals his aching desire to "go to the altar of God, to God my exceeding joy" (Psalm 43:4). A literal translation of this reference to God reads "to the God of the joy of my rejoicing."[7] Do you think of God as your "exceeding joy" or "the joy of your rejoicing"? Do you turn to Him, who lives in your heart, for joy? God—the only Source of true joy—wants to give you His joy. You need only to turn to Him to receive it.

Second, *God's salvation* is a great reason for joy. I'm sure you've noticed that when people explain how they became Christians, they can't help but tell their story joyfully! Isaiah, for instance, could not contain his joy when he thought about all that God had done for him. He wrote, "I will rejoice greatly in the Lord, my soul will exult in my God; for He has clothed me with garments of salvation, He has wrapped me with a robe of righteousness" (Isaiah 61:10). Because of the great price God paid to obtain our salvation through His Son's death, we are wise to regularly reflect on our salvation and what that means. Doing so in touch with the Source of joy.

Third, *God's promises* are another cause for great joy—and His promises are many. At one time, our family had a little plastic container shaped like a loaf of bread on our breakfast table. Each of the cards in that box had one promise from the Bible printed on it. Every morning one of us would close our eyes, reach over, pick a promise, and then read it as a part of our family devotions.

Later that night at supper we would talk about our promise-for-the-day again and how we had seen God be true to His Word since breakfast time. Beloved, your Bible is like that plastic loaf of bread: It is filled with promises—as many (according to one calculation) as 8,000![8]

My friend Mary uses God's promises to find joy in her life of chronic illness. She writes:

> My health problem frequently robs me of joy. I often find myself in despair, depression, self-pity, and other fleshly attitudes. This week, when troubled with my affliction, I focused on the Lord. When I prayed to see the good in my pain, I recalled various promises in Scripture. I was reminded that God is a God of comfort who comforts us in all our afflictions (2 Corinthians 1:3-4). It also helped to remember that God is in control and has a unique purpose for me (2 Timothy 1:9; Ephesians 1:11). He is using this affliction to work out His will for me—to help me be more Christlike—for my good and His glory (Romans 8:28). So I will keep on thanking Him for this [illness] daily, even though I may not fully understand the purpose behind it.

As Mary is learning, God's promises to us are a bottomless reservoir of joy which you and I can draw from at any moment by simply opening His Word and believing His promises. It's even better if you've memorized some of those promises and hidden them in your heart!

Fourth, *Christ's kingdom* is a reason for us to have joy in our lives. The fact that we who name Jesus as Savior and Lord have been welcomed into His kingdom brings great joy to the angels (Luke 15:10), and the news of souls coming to Christ should evoke joy in us as well. Such joy characterized the young church in Acts. Paul and Barnabas went from town to town describing in detail the conversion of the Gentiles, bringing great *joy* to all the brethren (Acts 15:3, emphasis added). I get a taste of this cause for joy during baptisms at my home church. Hearing each man and woman explain how God has changed their lives is truly a source of joy for me!

Finally, as we meet the challenges of life and deal with the pain that comes our way, *our future in Christ* should also bring us joy. Just like the reward we plan for ourselves to celebrate the end of a stressful season of life, we can look forward to our future in Christ—a future that holds not death, but everlasting life with God in heaven! Psalm 16:11 describes what that future will be like in the presence of God: "In Thy presence is *fullness of joy;* in Thy right hand there are *pleasures forever*" (emphasis added). Precious friend, when the trials of life seem unbearable and never-ending, you can look forward with great anticipation and assurance to your future home with God in heaven—where there shall no longer be any mourning, or crying, or pain (Revelation 21:4)—and experience deep joy despite earthly suffering.

Clearly the joy of the Lord is marvelously available to us twenty-four hours a day, every day, whatever we're dealing with! One seminary wife I know has gone back to work so that her husband can finish school. "Once when I was facing a whole day of work with many projects going," she remembers, "I was starting to feel overwhelmed and down, sorry for myself that I had to work. But God knew my ultimate desire to be fruitful, and the Holy Spirit prompted me to remember that, despite how I felt, I had access to great joy! So I ran to the Source and let God fill me with His joy until I was full."

Praise God that this fullness of joy is available to you and me, too! All we have to do is fix our focus on God—not our gloom; on the eternal—not the temporal. We experience the joy *of* the Lord when we go to Him and find our joy *in* the Lord. True joy—spiritual joy—is found only in the things of God. You and I cultivate the fruit of joy when we ask God to keep us walking with and abiding in Him. Ask God for His grace. Ask Him to help you remember in your times of need to go to Him to be filled with His joy.

An Image for Joy

One day my daughter Katherine received an unusual phone call from a business student at her college who was making print and video catalogs of diamonds. Steve had almost everything he needed to create his catalog—the diamonds, a studio, a camera, the lights. But he needed one more thing—a pair of hands. A friend of his at The Master's College had told him, "Katherine George has the most beautiful hands I've ever seen." Well, with that recommendation, Steve phoned Katherine.

So Katherine drove to downtown Los Angeles to model diamonds for Steve's catalogs. When she arrived at the studio, Steve set up his camera and lights. Then he opened his suitcase and pulled out a piece of black velvet that was to serve as a backdrop for the diamonds. After turning on his studio lights, he removed the diamonds from his case, one by one for Katherine to model.

Instructing Katherine to slowly lift her hand up off the dark background toward the light as she modeled each ring, Steve explained, "When a diamond is placed against a dark background, the darkness makes it seem more brilliant. And, when the diamond is lifted toward a light, all of its facets are revealed and allowed to sparkle. A diamond is pretty all by itself, but putting it against a black background and lifting it up to the light enhances its radiance and glory."

Oh, my friend! What a perfect picture of joy! True spiritual joy shines brightest against the darkness of trials, tragedy, and testing! And the blacker the background, the greater the brilliance. Similarly, life's dark struggles make Christian joy more intense and our heartfelt praise more glorious. As one writer has noted, God "setteth in pain the jewel of His joy."[9]

The Sacrifice of Praise

With that image in mind, I consider *the sacrifice of praise* a slogan that is helpful in cultivating the fruit of joy. Let me explain.

When life is good, praise and thanksgiving flow automatically from my heart and lips. But when life turns black, praise and thanksgiving don't flow quite so easily! Instead, I have to deliberately choose to follow God's advice and "in everything give thanks; for this is God's will for you in Christ Jesus" (1 Thessalonians 5:18). Although I don't *feel* like praising the Lord or thanking Him, I *do* what God says, and that effort makes my praise a sacrifice. When I'd rather bask in self-pity or stay stuck in my depression, choosing to look beyond my pain makes my praise to God sacrificial. But, when I do lift such a sacrifice of praise to God out of the darkness of my trials, I find the Spirit's joy magnified in my life—just as lifting a diamond to the light against a black background enhances its brilliance!

I'm learning to offer this sacrifice of praise when I'm in pain because God calls us to be joyful… *at all times* (Philippians 4:4)! And I'm glad He gives us flesh-and-blood models in His Word. For instance, in the Old Testament, King David worships in the house of the Lord despite the aggression of his enemies. Lifting his eyes away from his predicament and looking to God his Protector, David declares that—in spite of his difficulties—"I [will] offer in His tabernacle sacrifices of joy" (Psalm 27:6 KJV).

I need God's joy—I admit it! And I (and probably you as well) most need His joy when things are black. We both need joy when we're suffering and misunderstood, when we're rejected and hated, and when we're in emotional or physical pain. But our sacrifice of praise to God gives the Spirit room to touch us with His joy that overshadows these circumstances.

It's amazing to realize that, with the sacrifice of praise, the very hindrances to our joy become the soil out of which joy blossoms. Suffering, infirmities, affliction, pain, and loss create in us the need to go to God to receive His joy. Deprivation, stress, and the demands of life—a heavy schedule, a multitude of responsibilities—compel us to go to the Father. The Spirit uses our pain, sorrow, and grief to prompt us to lift before God a sacrifice of praise. Thus, we come in touch with the unshakable joy of the Lord!

And you, beloved? I know I've shared from my own life and struggles, but whatever your current circumstances, there's no better time than now for a prayer of praise to your loving and understanding Father. Why not allow the sweet aroma of your sacrifice to drift heavenward and God's gentle presence to comfort your soul? Allow your prayer to impress on you a greater awareness of His presence. You, too, can know fullness of joy in Him.

The Sounds of Joy

It's a well-known fact that the wife of preacher C.H. Spurgeon, Susannah Spurgeon, suffered from physical disabilities that grew progressively worse year by year. Finally she reached the point where she could no longer accompany him on his travels as often as she used to. Then, not only did she have to endure her painful affliction, but she also had to deal with C.H. Spurgeon's absence for weeks at a time. Read here what she wrote one dark, cold, lonely evening when she was sitting alone (it seemed she was always alone now) beside her fire:

> The fire was letting loose the imprisoned music from the old oak's inmost heart. [As] the fierce tongues of the flames came to consume [the log's hardened] callousness...the fire wrung from him a song and a sacrifice.

> Oh! Thought I, when the fire of affliction draws songs of praise from us, then indeed…our God is glorified!…We [would] give forth no melodious sounds were it not for the fire which kindles round us and releases tender notes of trust in Him.… Singing in the fire!…Let the furnace be heated seven times hotter than before![10]

Yes, precious friend, joy sings in the fire. Joy glorifies God through tears and pain. Joy spurs us to give thanks for God's goodness…even when circumstances are not good! Joy prompts the offering of the sacrifice of praise…even when life gives us no apparent reason to celebrate. Are these sounds of joy pouring out of *your* heart and lips? Ask God to bless you with joy in the Lord as you walk with Him through every day, o'er all the way.

Hannah's Song of Joy

Her daily life was hard and her circumstances dark, but Hannah, another woman who walked with God, nevertheless knew the brilliant joy of the Lord. As the Book of 1 Samuel opens, we learn right away that Elkanah had two wives, Hannah and Peninnah, "and Peninnah had children, but Hannah had no children" (1:2). Year after year, Peninnah flaunted her ability to bear children before Hannah, moving her to tears and prompting her to lose her appetite.

How would you cope with Peninnah's provocation if you were Hannah? And, more realistically, how are you handling what God is doing (or not doing!) in your life right now? Hannah has much to teach us.

Hannah quietly endured her pain. First, Hannah had no children and was therefore considered a failure and social embarrassment.[11] Furthermore, each day she suffered ill treatment from the woman with whom she shared her beloved husband. Then, when

Hannah went to the temple to pour out her heart to God, the high priest misread her agony as drunkenness (verse 13). Despite all this pain, we never read about words of anger or self-pity coming from Hannah's lips. She looked to the Lord rather than lashing out at her provoker or her husband.

Hannah never acted out of vengeance. We also don't hear of Hannah seeking retribution upon Peninnah or Elkanah. She didn't even ask her husband to stop Peninnah's ridicule! In fact, she didn't even tell him what was going on, a report which might have turned him against her rival.

Hannah sought God through prayer (1 Samuel 1:10-16). Instead of turning to others, Hannah turned to the Almighty, knowing that He was the *only* One who understood her difficulties and the *only* One who could do something about it. In these black days of her life, Hannah looked to God to be her source of hope and joy, lifting her problems to Him and hoping in His promises. Although she could have shared her pain with her husband, she didn't. Hannah was alone…except for God. For her, joy would come from God, and God alone!

Hannah rejoiced as she offered her son to God. As she cried out to God in prayer, Hannah vowed that, if He gave her a son, she would give him back to the Lord all the days of his life (1 Samuel 1:11). God Almighty answered her prayer and gave her Samuel. And, true to her word, Hannah then gave Him back her dear boy—probably at the tender age of three years old!

But Hannah's story doesn't end here. As this godly mother took her child to the tabernacle and prepared to say good-bye to him, she offered the sacrifice of praise along with the sacrifice of her son. Hannah prayed, "My heart rejoiceth in the Lord.…I rejoice in Thy salvation" (1 Samuel 2:1 KJV). You see, the source of Hannah's joy was God—*not* a human, *not* a child, *not* a son, *not* the long-prayed-for gift God had given her.

Doesn't this sobering look at Hannah's life call for us to take a personal inventory? For instance, what is God asking you to endure as you walk oh-so-closely to Him? Is pain coming from many directions? And how are you treating the people causing or aggravating your pain? Is your spirit vengeful, your tongue angry and spiteful? Are you enduring the hardship quietly? Are you allowing these hard times to press you to prayer, to fasting, to turning daily to God's Word, to worshiping weekly with His people? Are you seeking God with all your heart, soul, strength, and mind (Luke 10:27)? Do you know that you can find joy in God? Joy in the Lord can be yours—right this moment!—as you offer up to Him the sacrifice of praise.

The Supreme Model of Joy

Jesus Himself gives us the supreme model of joy in the midst of life's dark pain. There was probably no greater source of pain in the ancient world than crucifixion on a Roman cross, but we read in Hebrews 12:2 that Jesus, "for the joy set before Him endured the cross, despising the shame." Knowing that His suffering would result in great joy, Jesus looked toward His future with the Father as He endured the excruciating pain of death on the cross. As one commentator notes, "Despite the misunderstanding, the rejection, the hatred, the pain He endured from men while incarnate among them, the Lord never lost His joy in the relationship He had with His Father. And that joy He gives to each of His followers."[12] The same wondrous joy that Jesus experienced in His darkest hours is yours and mine today. Won't you look to God for that joy? Let it help you endure your dark and pain-filled days.

Cultivating Joy

Now, my friend, what can you and I do to cultivate this fruit of joy in the Lord in our daily walk with God?

• Offer the sacrifice of praise to God continually—even

when you don't feel like it (Hebrews 13:15). Through the power of the Holy Spirit, this act of thanksgiving transforms our pain into praise.

- "Consider it all joy…when you encounter various trials," writes James (1:2). As I said earlier, let the very hindrances to joy become the soil out of which joy blossoms! That happens when we let life's hard times drive us nearer to the Lord, the only Source of genuine joy and real hope.

- Give thanks in everything (1 Thessalonians 5:18).

- Whatever is happening—good or bad—give thanks to God for His sovereignty, His perfect timing, His perfect plan, and His unconditional love.

- Bless the Lord at all times (Psalm 34:1). Offer unceasingly the sacrifice of praise (Hebrews 13:15). The Spirit can—and will—use your praise to touch you with God's joy.

- Focus on the reality of God's promises. Every time you open your Bible, read with a marker in hand and look for powerful promises that can change your outlook to one of joy. Go a step further and memorize those verses you like best and meditate on them.

- Look up. Shift your eyes and your hopes away from your suffering and focus instead on the splendor of God (Psalm 121:1-2).

- Obey God's command to be joyful always (1 Thessalonians 5:16). As author Jerry Bridges notes, "We are not to sit around waiting for our circumstances to make us joyful. We are commanded to be joyful always…we should continually be growing in joy."[13]

- Go to God to be filled with His joy whenever you need it.

Assignment for Joy

My heart hurts as I ask this question, dear friend, knowing that until we are with the Lord there will always be suffering… but what trial is causing you the greatest grief, the sharpest pain, the deepest sorrow today? Is it a physical affliction or terminal disease, an unbelieving husband, the loss of a home or a job, the deterioration of finances or health, the breakdown of a family, the turning away of a child? Is it a disappointment, a dashed dream, a disaster or disability? Is it ridicule or persecution? A difficult season as a wife or mother, daughter or daughter-in-law? Is it a strained relationship somewhere or an unknown future as you look down the road of life? Whatever your greatest trial today, let it move you to God, compel you to offer Him a sacrifice of praise, and so enable you to be touched by Him, the only Source of true joy.

Things to Do Today to Walk in Joy

1. As we discussed previously, identify the trial that causes you the greatest grief.

2. Faithfully offer to God the sacrifice of your praise (Hebrews 13:15)…even if it is offered with tears.

3. Consider that trial a joy for what God can do in your life as a result of it (see James 1:2-4 and Romans 5:1-5).

4

Experiencing God's Peace

❧

The fruit of the Spirit is...peace.

GALATIANS 5:22

Newspaper columnist and counselor Ann Landers received an average of 10,000 letters each month, nearly all of them from people with problems. When asked if any one problem stood out in the mail she received, she said the greatest problem seems to be fear—people's fear of losing their health, their wealth, and their loved ones.

The medical profession sees the same fear in people. Despite what patients themselves say, the vast majority of all chronic patients today have one common symptom. In 90 percent of these cases, the first symptom was *not* a cough or chest pain, but fear...which sooner or later manifested itself in some sort of clinical symptom.

Causes for fear surround us on every side, but as Christians, dear sister, you and I have still another built-in resource for handling these fears. That resource is the peace of God, the next fruit on Paul's list of Christian graces. And what a refreshing fruit that peace is in a mad, mad, mad, mad world! In our roller-coaster society that offers no guarantees, we who are God's children can experience His peace—no matter what is happening in our life—when we walk by His Spirit. As we are blessed with the peace of God in the midst of life's trials, we experience a new closeness to Him.

Understanding the Peace of the Lord

What exactly is this peace that God's Spirit gives? Many people think of peace as the absence of problems, as the feeling that is experienced when all is well. But the peace of the Lord is not related to circumstances at all. In fact, God's peace comes to us and endures…regardless of life's circumstances.

At one time our Courtney and Paul lived on Kauai, Hawaii, the island which experienced the ravages of Hurricane Iniki in 1992. As Jim and I drove around the island on a visit, we noticed not only the remaining evidence of destruction, but also the huge warning sirens on every beach and in every town. Having just been through a 6.7 earthquake in Southern California, we could well imagine something of the fear the islanders must have felt as those sirens wailed on that fateful September day. But we could also imagine the peace they must have felt when those same devices finally sounded the all-clear signal. But, can you imagine having perfect peace when the sirens are signaling a storm or when the hurricane is actually roaring around you? That, my friend, is the kind of peace God makes available to you and me for the storms of life. Notice these truths about this peace that comes from God.

- Our peace has nothing to do with our circumstances, and everything to do with knowing we have a right relationship with God.[1]

- Our peace has nothing to do with daily challenges or crises, and everything to do with knowing that our times are in God's hands.[2]

- Our peace has nothing to do with the conditions of our life, and everything to do with knowing that God is all-sufficient.[3]

- Our peace is an inward repose[4] and serenity of soul[5] that indicates a heart at rest—regardless of our circumstances—as we place complete confidence in God minute by minute.

True spiritual peace comes with *knowing that our heavenly Father is continually with us*—and indeed He is! God is omnipresent and therefore fully aware of every detail of our life—at every moment and in every place. He knows our needs—at all times and in every situation. As Psalm 139:7-12 teaches, we can never be anyplace—from the heights of heaven to the depths of the sea—where God is not present with us and available to us. Key to our peace, then, is not the *absence* of conflict, but the *presence* of God, no matter what the conflict.[6] I have to tell you that just *writing* about God's personal and continuous presence is bringing a fresh sense of peace to my soul right this minute!

Peace also comes with *acknowledging that God will supply our every need* as well as acknowledging His constant presence. For instance, when Paul asked Jesus to remove the thorn in his flesh and Jesus said no, the apostle Paul learned the truth of Jesus' statement: "My grace is sufficient for you" (2 Corinthians 12:9). Paul learned for himself the truth he wrote in Philippians 4:19— "God [will] supply all your needs according to His riches in glory in Christ Jesus"—and, in 2 Corinthians 9:8, that "God is able to make all grace abound to you, that always having all sufficiency in everything, you may have an abundance for every good deed." Do you realize what these promises mean to you and me? They mean that we will never have a real need that God is not able to meet. What a reason for peace that truth is!

Trusting God

But to enjoy God's peace, we have to actively trust Him. Jesus stated as a fact, "In the world you have tribulation" (John 16:33). But as Christians who abide in Christ there is peace (even in tribulation!) as we rest in God's presence and trust in His promises. When you and I walk by the Spirit, our life is characterized *not* by fretting, panic, and anxiety, but by the quiet peace that comes with trusting God. In the midst of life's most difficult circumstances, the Spirit's peace will guard our hearts and our minds" (Philippians 4:7), serving as a sentinel over our thoughts and emotions...despite life's turbulence.

I think of peace as *the sacrifice of trust*. And you and I make the sacrifice of trust when we face the painful and distressing realities of our life and then choose to trust God instead of panicking or falling apart. When circumstances in my life might tempt me to panic, feel terrified, become a nervous wreck, or be filled with dread, I can choose either to give in to those feelings or to trust in God and present myself to Him to be filled with His peace. And I must make this conscious choice each and every day whenever I see storm clouds looming ahead, whenever life's confusions, bewilderments, and perplexities threaten to overwhelm. You see, I can either trust Almighty God or succumb to the emotions of the flesh. Choosing to trust God—making the sacrifice of trust—causes me to experience His peace...even in the midst of tremendous uproar. We make the sacrifice of trust and experience God's peace...

> when we choose not to panic...but to rest in God's
> presence,
> when we release our terror...and trust in God's
> wisdom and ways,

when we reject our nervousness…and remember
    that God is in control,
and when we ignore our dread…and instead
    accept God's dealings.

Receiving God's Peace

When we are filled with His Spirit and walking in His ways, we have instant access to "the peace of God, which surpasses all comprehension" (Philippians 4:7). And that peace which comes from God—and from Him alone—comes to us through four gifts He has given to us.

God, the Son —First of all, you and I have peace through the gift of Jesus Christ, God's Son. Seven hundred years before Jesus was born in a manger in Bethlehem, the Old Testament prophet Isaiah predicted, "For a child will be born to us, a son will be given to us…and His name will be called…Prince of Peace" (Isaiah 9:6). That name, dear sister, reflects His mission. Jesus' advent to earth accomplished our salvation. His death on Calvary gave us the gift of peace with God that comes only with forgiveness for our sins: "Having been justified by faith, we have peace with God through our Lord Jesus Christ" (Romans 5:1). Our personal peace with God comes through the work of God's Son on the cross.

God, the Father —A second gift our loving God has given us is the gift of knowing Him. In the Bible, we learn all about His promises and His faithfulness so that we may trust Him in our times of need. One of those promises is found in Isaiah 26:3: "Thou wilt keep him in perfect peace, whose mind is stayed on Thee, because he trusteth in Thee" (KJV). We certainly cannot avoid strife as we walk in the world, but we can know perfect peace in the midst of turmoil as we turn to God Himself instead of focusing on our difficulties.

God's Word—The Bible is another one of God's gifts that helps us know God by revealing His law, His ways, and His purposes. When we know and love and follow God's Word, we experience God's peace to the point that *nothing* causes us to stumble (Psalm 119:165)! When you and I embrace God's Word as our standard for living and obey His commands, we experience the peace which comes with maintaining a right relationship with God.

God, the Spirit —The Holy Spirit is our personal Helper, Teacher, and Comforter (John 14:26), and the instruction, guidance, and comfort we receive from Him are indeed gifts of peace. When we abide in Christ and walk by His Spirit, we receive this peace from God.

Clearly then, as Christians, we can look to God—the Father, the Son, and the Holy Spirit—and to God's Word for peace.

Choosing the Peace of God over Panic

It's amazing to me how many situations in ordinary life can cause panic, terror, dread, fear, or doubt. For example, considering the responsibility of providing for a family or wondering about our children's safety can cause panic. For many, the memory of abuse or the anticipation of further harm can trigger dread. Terror can come with submitting to a biopsy, facing surgery, or hearing a cancer diagnosis. Pain and death can bring about fear and doubt. Danger stirs up all these emotions—as I learned during the Northridge earthquake of 1995 and its continuing aftershocks.

Such everyday causes for fear are a part of the lives of many women I know. My heart—and prayers—went out to the student who wrote me the following note:

> I've been contemplating having a medical test done
> for some pains I've had in my stomach. These past

two weeks the pains have increased, so I've scheduled the test for this Friday. Because I am prone to
diagnose my case and I wonder about all the things
it could be, my mind becomes restless and distracted, and panic sets in.

At our weekly Bible study, another woman shared that she
was struggling with fear because her husband had been laid off
from his job for three months and had no work or income. She
asked us to pray that she would continue to choose to rest in
God's peace and in the fact that He is in complete control of their
situation.

Yes, the events of everyday life can indeed cause panic, terror,
dread, fear, and doubt. At such times, we definitely need God's
peace; and our Savior readily gives us His peace when, in those
moments, we choose to trust Him. As writer and speaker Elisa-
beth Elliot shares, you and I must trust God "up to the fingernail-
scraping edge." Praise God that we can weather the panic-causing
situations of life by trusting in Him, resting in the fact that our
times are in His hands, and placing our complete confidence in
His all-sufficiency!

Jesus' disciples were fortunate to witness His all-sufficiency in
a situation which understandably caused them to panic. Here's
what happened: After a long day of teaching, Jesus and the Twelve
got into a boat to travel to the other side of the lake. Luke reports
that, "as they were sailing along...a fierce gale of wind descended
upon the lake, and they began to be swamped and to be in danger" (Luke 8:23). As the waves broke over the boat and began to
fill it with water (Mark 4:37), Jesus was asleep! The peace of God
did indeed surpass all comprehension at this point! How could
Jesus sleep in such a storm? Didn't He feel the turbulence? Didn't
He know He could lose His life right there in the Sea of Galilee?

While the disciples panicked, Jesus remained calm. Jesus'

peace came from His knowledge that His times were in the Father's hands. You see, Jesus trusted, and therefore Jesus rested. He knew that He wasn't going to die one second before God's scheduled time and that if now was His time to die, nothing could prevent it. Abiding in the Father, Jesus had complete confidence in the power and sufficiency of God.

What a sharp contrast Jesus' response is when compared with that of His faithful (or faithless?) followers! Their panic was revealed in their wake-up call to Jesus—"Master, Master, we are perishing!" (Luke 8:24). As the wind howled and the waves crashed, Jesus said to them, "Where is your faith?" (Luke 8:25). And Jesus would probably ask this same question of you and me when we find ourselves panicking. How little the disciples then— and you and I today!—seem to trust in Jesus.

It's plain to see that you and I need to remember something that the disciples didn't: Our days are in God's hands. Our God is all-sufficient to meet our needs, and the Savior is with us every step of the way. And just as the disciples could have rested if they had trusted, we can experience the peace of God when we offer the sacrifice of trust. Panic is needless, wasted energy, and stewing, fretting, and worrying signal a failure to trust our faithful Father. But when we choose to trust God, we can have the same peace in God that Christ had in the storm at sea and in many other scenes from His life. Our Jesus, even when He was threatened with death, confronted by enemies, and walking to the cross, rested in God and always acknowledged that His times were in God's hands and that His all-sufficient Father would meet His every need.

Well, dear reader, can *you* trust God this way? Can you let Him, His Son, His Word, and His Holy Spirit be channels of peace? Will you trust in God as soon as a reason to panic arises? By turning to God at just such a moment, you allow the Holy Spirit to fill you with His peace as you walk through trying times.

Choosing the Peace of God When Pressure Mounts

Perhaps even more prevalent in our lives than reasons to panic are sources of pressure. We never seem to have enough time—pressure! We want to do well as a spouse and a parent—pressure! We are called to be good stewards of finances and effective managers of a home—pressure! Jobs, friendships, responsibilities to aging parents, health problems, and even service at church—all of these bring on pressure and too easily squeeze out the peace of God.

We can thank the Lord that as we live in the whirlwind of life and the flurry of daily demands, His peace is available to us. We don't have to live in a frazzled fashion—breathless, anxious, worried, fretful, and rushed. But how?

Do you remember when Jesus went to the home of Mary and Martha? Martha welcomed Him (and probably His twelve hungry disciples) in for dinner, but she "was distracted with all her preparations" (Luke 10:40) and soon let the mounting pressure she felt to fix the meal rob her of any peace—a fact that became quite obvious.

First, *Martha's manner* was a dead giveaway. Her behavior has been described as cumbered, distracted, worried, and busy.[7] She tensely scurried about, bustling and bothered, fretting and fuming, a picture of anxiety in motion. She was literally—and breathlessly—caught up in the whirlwind of life. The cook herself was in a stew, whipping herself up into a froth. Finally, no longer able to handle the pressure, she "burst in" (verse 40, PHILLIPS)[8] with a few words for Jesus!

That's when *Martha's mouth* revealed her lack of peace. "Lord, do You not care...?" she asked the Master accusingly (verse 40). Pointing the finger of blame at Mary, Martha next said, "She has left me to do all the serving alone." The bossy big sister then dared to tell the Lord what to do: "Tell her to help me." Yes, besides stirring up a meal in the kitchen, Martha certainly stirred up quite a commotion in the living room with her verbal outburst!

Martha's confusion about *her mission* also robbed her of peace. She was right to be serving Jesus, but she mistakenly thought that *serving* was her primary mission. Jesus saw the confused priorities of this well-intentioned woman and commented, "Martha, Martha, you are worried and bothered about so many things" (verse 41). In her efforts to serve God, Martha failed to remember that "man's chief end is to glorify God and enjoy Him forever."[9]

So at last we come to *Martha's mindset* and the priorities which kept her from knowing God's peace: Martha was preoccupied with details and secondary issues.[10] Her service to Jesus had degenerated into mere busywork that was removed from any devotion to Him. And this focus on service rather than on the One she was serving prompted Jesus to instruct her by pointing out that her sister Mary had chosen "the good part" (verse 42) by sitting at Jesus' feet, listening to His Word, and abiding in His presence. (Oh, how many times I myself have acted like Martha!)

Now, what can we learn from Martha's sister? First of all, Mary rested at the Lord's feet while Martha was restless. She also worshiped the Lord while Martha worried about the meal. She knew the peace of the presence of God while Martha panicked at a distance. *Mary's manner* clearly revealed a soul at rest and "the imperishable quality of a gentle and quiet spirit, which is precious in the sight of God" (1 Peter 3:4).

And *Mary's mouth* rested, too. Sitting in the presence of God Himself, she had much to learn. You see, Jesus spoke the words of life...and so Mary was quiet.

Like her sister, *Mary's mission* was also to serve, but she also understood the more important priority of worship. Wanting her relationship with Jesus to be the highest priority of her life, Mary made choices which reflected that desire. She knew when to quit serving...and start sitting.

Clearly, *Mary's mindset* was pleasing to the Lord. As Jesus said, Mary had "chosen the good part, which shall not be taken away from her" (verse 42). She had her mind set on things above, not on earthly things (Colossians 3:2). She was focused on the eternal, not the temporal (2 Corinthians 4:18).

I know Mary is definitely a model *I* need for my hurricane lifestyle and, I'm guessing, a model you need, too! And so I try to remember this picture of Mary sitting… resting…worshiping…at peace…as I plan another wedding, start the messy process of remodeling after the earthquake, face a book deadline, and juggle the continuing everyday demands of schedules, commitments, and life.

And now it's time for a closer look at your own manner, mouth, mission, and mindset. What would an outside observer see in you right now—a Martha or a Mary? Are you in turmoil, or are you trusting and at peace? Are you running around in circles, or are you resting in the Lord? Are your words revealing a sense of panic and pressure, or are they words that edify and encourage, that minister grace to those who hear (Ephesians 4:29)? Are your actions reflecting the priorities God would have you set? Is your relationship with Him first, or are you too busy to sit at His feet and enjoy His presence? The woman who wrote the following words knew busyness…until the Lord interrupted. Let's learn from her.

I'm Busy, Lord!

I'm busy, Lord. Surely You can see
The thousand things that wait for me!
The dishes still lie in the sink—
I cannot stop to pray and think.

Lord, I know You understand,
For You gave these children to my hand;
And now they cry and need me so,
Lord, You understand. I'd better go.

Now I've got them all to sleep,
I'd better dust and mop and sweep.
I must thaw out the meat for stew,
And the ironing is long overdue!

And kindly my Lord answered me,
"Why do you from My presence flee?
I have so much for you today.
My child, I want to hear you pray.

"I love you, child; I want you here
To rest and listen—to shed a tear.
What if Paul had stopped to say,

'Lord, I'm too busy to write letters today!'?

"No, my child, I'm what you need,
Through household duties you can speed,
Yet when you're through, there's emptiness
If this quiet time you miss."

Oh, thank You, Lord, for showing me
How much I need to wait on Thee.
For what's an undone dish or two
Compared with sharing time with You?!

—Nancy Stitzel

May God enable us like Mary and like Nancy, the author of this poem, to choose to make our number one priority "the good part which shall not be taken away"—our relationship with Him!

Walking on the Path of Peace

Well, dear one, now that we know more about God's peace, what can you and I do to live in such a way that we can cultivate this gift of His Spirit?

- We can *pray!* And we should pray first, pray often, pray continually. When we come to God in prayer and place our worries, fears, doubts, and concerns into His hands, we can be more like Mary. We'll be spending time in the presence of the Lord, enjoying fellowship with Him, learning from Him, and worshiping Him—and, yes, experiencing His peace.

- We can *pause* and turn to the Lord when a crisis or catastrophe presents itself. When we pause to acknowledge God—His presence, His all-sufficiency, His power, His love—He will make our paths straight. Furthermore, once we've turned to Him, we will again be in touch with His peace that passes understanding.

- We can *peruse* the Gospels and study Jesus' life to see the peace He experienced in stressful situations. We can learn how abiding in the Father directed Jesus' thoughts, words, deeds, responses, and reactions in difficult circumstances. We can carry these instances in our mind and write them on the tablet of our heart so that we can follow the example of our Savior.

Things to Do Today to Walk in Peace

Do you know what challenge causes you to most act like Martha? What worry keeps you awake at night? What concern sets your mind and heart fretting as the alarm clock awakens you each morning? Please identify that item, dear one, and then make the conscious decision to trust it to God. Making this sacrifice of trust will allow *your* heart to rest in Him and enable *you* to experience His peace—even in your most difficult challenge!

5

Looking at Jesus' Attitudes

The preceding three chapters of this book, dear friend, have been about the circumstances of life that call for you and me to display the fruits of love, joy, and peace. First, the need for *love* is created by ill treatment, hostility, abuse, and hatred. Second, the need for *joy* springs from sorrow, tribulation, tragedy, affliction, and trials. Third, the need for *peace* comes as we face the events in life that evoke panic, fear, terror, dread, and anxiety. Oh, but how blessed you and I are to be able to follow the example of Jesus Christ, who faced these same fruit-bearing opportunities! We've already seen Jesus model each of the attitudes of love, joy, and peace. But now I want us to take a close look at Jesus in the Garden of Gethsemane, where we see Him living out all three attitudes...despite the events He faced.

As I was preparing to write this chapter, I found these words written by pastor John MacArthur:

> Ever and always the teacher, Jesus used even this struggle with the enemy in the garden the night

> before the cross to teach the disciples and every
> future believer another lesson in godliness, a lesson
> about facing temptation and severe trial. The Lord
> not only was preparing Himself for the cross but
> also, by His example, preparing His followers for
> the crosses He calls them to bear in His name....[1]

Because you and I desire to walk in godliness, let's allow Jesus to teach us as we peer into this dark night—a physically dark night that was also the most spiritually dark night in human history as the sinless Son faced death for your sins and mine in order to accomplish our salvation.

As we look at this sacred scene from the Savior's life, you and I truly stand on holy ground! Jesus' life on earth is nearing its end and He faces every ugly word and evil deed ever directed at a person. Through God's provision of the four Gospels, you and I are allowed to witness exactly how Jesus handled this hatred, sorrow, and trauma.

The Plan

Throughout His three years of teaching, Jesus often referred to God's plan for His death, which always caused bewilderment in His disciples. For instance, in John 7:6 Jesus said, "My time [to die] is not yet at hand." But in Matthew 26, as Jesus prepared for His final Passover meal, He clearly stated the opposite: "My time *is* at hand" (verse 18, emphasis added). It was time for Him to die and to fulfill the Father's plan.

Jesus and His small band of followers were in Jerusalem to observe the Passover, and together they supped one final time. Judas the traitor had already been dismissed to do the evil deed of betraying his Master and it was nearing midnight on Thursday of the Passover week.[2] At this time, Jesus offered His high priestly prayer for and with His disciples (John 17). Then the group sang a hymn (Matthew 26:30) and Jesus "went forth with His disciples over the ravine of the Kidron, where there was a garden, into which He Himself entered, and His disciples" (John 18:1).

The Purpose

What was it that drove Jesus to the Garden of Gethsemane? It was His situation. It was this crossroads in His life. It was the challenge He faced during His final days. His time had finally come—and what was ahead? Betrayal by His disciples. Misunderstanding from His family and followers. Rejection from mankind. Hostility and persecution. An angry mob, angry leaders, and angry people. Verbal and physical assault. An unjust sentence. The excruciating pain of crucifixion. Death. And, worst of all, momentary separation from His heavenly Father. From the human perspective, Jesus was losing all He had: His life, His family, His ministry, His friends, and His personal dignity.

Yet, His heavenly Father had commanded that He die for these sinners, and Jesus obeyed. Doing so would benefit others—including you and me!—because His death would be for sinners like us. So, acting in love, Jesus gave Himself as a sacrifice, a ransom for others (Matthew 20:28).

The Place

Facing the overwhelming challenge of the cross, Jesus went to Gethsemane (Matthew 26:36). This place was probably a secluded spot, walled in and containing some olive trees and perhaps a grotto used in the fall of the year for an olive oil-press.[3] Jesus had gone there often with His disciples (John 18:2) because it was quiet, a good spot for teaching, prayer, rest, and sleep. So, on the eve of His death, Jesus retreated to this familiar place of prayer with His little band of followers.

The People

After He entered the place called Gethsemane, Jesus did two things. First, He asked eight of the disciples to "sit here while I go over there and pray" (Matthew 26:36). Jesus left these men outside the wall or gate of the garden as sentries. Next Jesus invited three of the disciples—Peter, James, and John—to go along with Him to pray.

The Problems

Disappearing into the black darkness, Jesus began the battle. The Father's plan caused Him deep distress, and the Bible gives us glimpses into His extensive *emotional* anguish. Jesus cried out, "My soul is deeply grieved, to the point of death" (Matthew 26:38). He "began to be very distressed and troubled" (Mark 14:33), so much so that He fell upon the ground in prayer. Luke tells us that He was "in agony" (22:44). Our Lord "offered up both prayers and supplications with loud crying and tears" (Hebrews 5:7). As one commentator writes, "All the waves and the billows of distress came pouring over His soul."[4]

God's command to die also caused Jesus to suffer not only emotional turmoil, but also terrible *physical* stress: "Being in agony He was praying very fervently; and His sweat became like drops of blood, falling down upon the ground" (Luke 22:44).

Jesus was fighting another great battle in addition to these emotional and physical struggles, and that was the *spiritual* war. Knowing this, Jesus had instructed His companions, "Keep watching and praying, that you may not enter into temptation" (Matthew 26:41). Our Lord threw Himself upon the mercy of His Father and uttered, "My Father, if it is possible, let this cup [of death] pass from Me" (verse 39). On the physical level, Jesus wanted the cup to pass. No one has ever desired to taste death, and neither did Jesus. But, from the spiritual perspective, He wanted to do His Father's will and therefore added to His plea, "yet not as I will, but as Thou wilt" (verse 39).

The Process

With this submission to God's will, we see Jesus emerge triumphant from His agonizing struggle in the Garden. How did He gain the victory? How did Jesus remain steadfast in the love, joy, and peace that compelled Him to die willingly for sinners and not give in to physical and emotional desires? What was the process? And what can you and I learn so that we, too, can grow in love, joy, and peace?

As we've seen before, *love is the sacrifice of self.* For love, Jesus looked to God, the Father, who had commanded Jesus the Son to die for sinners. And in love, Jesus looked to the Father, reached out to Him for His sustaining and strengthening love, and then, offering *the sacrifice of self,* determined to do the Father's will. Jesus' love looked to the Father—and looked at us—and the Spirit enabled Him to submit to death on a cross (Hebrews 9:14). The *flesh* wanted the cup to pass, but *love* looked to the Father and said, "Not my will, but Thine be done" (Matthew 26:39 KJV). That decision led to severe and intense suffering.

Joy offers the sacrifice of praise. In joy, Jesus lifted praise to God. Scripture tells us that Jesus experienced great joy: "for the joy that was set before Him [in the Father and by the Father, He] endured the cross, despising the shame" (Hebrews 12:2).

Peace comes with the sacrifice of trust. For peace, Jesus left His problems with God. "The peace that passeth all understanding" rushed to guard Jesus' heart and mind, and He got up off that holy, tear-stained, sweat-drenched ground to go on in peace, knowing His times were in the Father's hands, saying in all peace and with total trust, "Let us be going" (Matthew 26:46).

The Product

And now please note: Nothing about Jesus' circumstances changed! After agonizing in prayer, He was *still* going to go to the cross, *still* going to be crucified, *still* going to die, but He went to the cross sustained by God's love, joy, and peace.

And note something else: This transformation, this acceptance, this turning point was not accomplished with a snap of Jesus' finger, the wink of His eye, or the wave of any wand. It came because Jesus went to the Father—in agony and with blood and sweat and tears. Lying prostrate on the earth in literal darkness as He fought the deeper darkness that settled upon His soul, Jesus looked to His Father for the Father's love, the Father's joy, and the Father's peace. As a few lines of poetry read,

> And when there seems no chance, no change,
> From grief can set me free,
> Hope finds its strength in helplessness,
> And calmly waits for Thee.[5]

No, Jesus' ultimate submission to God's will did not come easily. One time in prayer was not enough (Matthew 26:39). Twice was not enough (verse 42). Jesus turned to the Father three separate times (verse 44). And these three times in prayer were not the flinging of trite thoughts toward heaven! They were more than likely three hourlong sessions (Matthew 26:40) of agonizing, wrestling, struggling, and fighting so that He could do all that God required of Him.

When our Savior finally rose to go forward and face the cross, He did so with love, with joy, and with peace. Filled with these graces, the Son was able to say, "Let us be going" (Mark 14:42).

The Performance

Oh, dear sister in Christ! You and I have just seen Jesus submit to His Father's will—to death on the cross! We cannot help but to ponder, to marvel! This is too amazing for us not to pause…and to praise…and to pray! Oh, dear Jesus, thank You!

But we must also look to ourselves and to our walk with the Father. How is our performance when it comes to following God's direction for our life? Speaking for myself, I know I pray so little. When something tough comes along in my day, I too often blurt out, "No way!" and go on my merry way. If something requires more than I want to give, I say, "Oh, thank you very much, but I won't be able to do that." Or I grind on, doing what I have to do—on my own, in my own flesh, and by my own power—never approaching the Father for His filling. I murmur, gripe, complain, and fret. I do my duty…but I do it grudgingly.

In times like these, I need to follow my Lord's example and go to my Garden of Gethsemane, my place of prayer. I need to turn to the Father and contend with my flesh until I realize His fruit of love, joy, and peace. I need to spend the time—however long it takes!—to allow Him to fill me with Himself until I have all of Him and He has all of me.

If you and I would, for one week or even one day, fellow follower, commit ourselves to God in this way—if we would commit ourselves to rush to Him in prayer and remember His promises when we need love, when we need joy, and when we need peace, and stay there until we have it, however long it takes—we could indeed change our world for Christ. If we would commit ourselves to spend time in the garden with the Father and to pay the price Christ paid to walk by the Spirit, overcome the flesh, and thereby experience God's love and joy and peace—well, the effects are unknown, untold, limitless! Prayer in our own garden would mean Christ in us changing our hearts, our marriages, our families, our homes, our neighborhoods, our world. And *He* can do it. But without *Him,* we can do nothing (John 15:5). Without Him, we only go through the motions, giving so little to a husband, a child, or a world that needs so much.

May my personal prayer for growth in these three attitudes of love, joy, and peace become your prayer as we visit the garden often as we walk along life's way…

> It is in prayer, Father,
> That we press ourselves to You,
> O All-Sufficient One,
> That we get…in order to give,
> that we petition…in order to praise,
> that we wrestle…in order to rest.
> We must have our time in the Garden.
> We must go to Gethsemane…
> daily…first…often, if need be.
> May we hold high in our hearts and minds
> this picture of Jesus in the Garden.
> Impress it upon our souls.
> May we follow in His steps
> and refuse to rise until we have
> Your love…Your joy…Your peace.
> We pray in Jesus' name, who has taught us how
> to pray. Amen.

ACTIONS
of the
Fruit of the Spirit

6

Resisting in Patience

❧

The fruit of the Spirit is...patience.

GALATIANS 5:22

E ach day in my own walk with God, I probably attempt the same thing you do: I try to design an ideal schedule that will guarantee me a devotional time with God, in His Word and in prayer, each morning. On a good day, when the alarm clock goes off in the morning, I hop out of bed full of good intentions and solid plans, and I experience Victory #1: I got up!

It feels so good to be up and in control of my day (so far, anyway!). What a blessing it is to enter into God's presence, revel in His Word, and linger in prayer; to settle the circumstances of my life with God before my day's responsibilities begin. And then I experience Victory #2: I had my quiet time!

Next I start going about my housekeeping chores—joyfully unloading the dishwasher, eagerly watering those impatiens, and lovingly straightening the house. Usually this happy spiritual condition extends to taking coffee and juice to Jim in bed, fixing his breakfast and lunch with a hum, and helping him load the car. After giving him a big hug and a kiss, I stand in the driveway and wave an enthusiastic "good-bye" as he drives away. Yes, I experience Victory #3: I got my husband off to work without any problems! He's happy, and I'm happy. I think to myself, "This is great! All is well! I'm on a roll. What a wonderful day this is going to be!"

But then real life—the rest of the day—begins. I remember when I was a young mother, and real life was dealing with two preschool daughters all day long. Later, real life meant managing teenagers...who soon became two more adults living in our home. And every mother knows that child-raising itself brings not only joys, but many sorrows as well.

Also, in real life the phone rings (a lot!), and I have to attend to the person and details of each call. Most calls go well. But then there are those problem calls. Someone's upset with me. Or the person on the phone says something that hurts me. Sometimes the caller reports something someone *else* has said or gives me some new information that demands a response or a decision. I may learn that I've been removed from some position or been rejected in some way.

Pain comes in a variety of packages—through a letter in the mail or a visitor to your house or by telephone. And when the "package" is opened, you and I are left confused, wounded, bewildered, baffled, and hurting. We may feel used or abused, dumped on or manipulated, heartsick or sorrowful. There was an insult, an accusation, a disagreement, an argument, a criticism, maybe even a physical blow or a lawsuit. Now what are we supposed to do?

Facing Up to the Challenge of People

When I came out of my prayer closet, the circumstances of my life were in order: I had laid before God the difficult situations of my life. I had nurtured and cultivated the attitudes of godliness there in my quiet time by drinking in God's Word and communing with Him in prayer until His Spirit had given me God's love, God's joy, and God's peace. I was ready to face life for one more day.

But—as the saying goes—where there are people, there are problems! So what can you and I do about people? How can we handle the people who cause us pain? How can we obtain Victory #4 and live in a manner that glorifies God? How can we continue to walk by the Spirit and not succumb to the flesh when we are assaulted by people?

Handling people in a gracious, Christlike manner presents a real test for us. But thank God that He gives us three more graces, three more fruit—patience, kindness, and goodness (Galatians 5:22)—for managing the strain of personal relationships. Love, joy, and peace are godly attitudes that enable us to handle the difficult circumstances of life. Patience, kindness, and goodness help us in our relationships with difficult people. One commentator noted this logical progression and wrote, "If an individual is strong in the love, joy, and peace of God, he will be able to reach out to his neighbor in a more Christlike manner."[1] Beloved, reaching out to others requires that we take action—the actions of patience, kindness, and goodness as we walk by the Spirit.

Our Calling to Patience

It's good to realize up front that as Christians you and I are called by God to be patient. God's Word instructs us to *"put on* a heart of...patience" (Colossians 3:12, emphasis added). We are to *adorn* ourselves with a heart of patience. Just as we dress our body every day by putting on clothes, we are to *dress* our spirit each morning with the godly quality of patience. How lovely to be robed with God's patience!

In addition to putting on a heart of patience, we are to *"walk*

...with patience" (Ephesians 4:1-2, emphasis added). In describing the Christian life, Paul writes that we can enhance our relationships with other believers and promote the unity of the church if we conduct our lives with patience. In other words, when we see faults in other people or are annoyed by them in any way, when we want to be irritated or critical and lash out, we are to be patient instead.

Although not easy, this is a practical first step to getting along with people—as Kelly certainly realized while on jury duty. She shared that

> ...showing patience has been an everyday struggle for me while serving with a group of jurors. Some of these people are inconsiderate and unkind, and it's very easy to get mad and upset with one another. But I am learning to deal with this situation in prayer. Every time something happens which starts to test my patience, I go to God and pray that He would give me the strength to overcome my impatience and anxious attitude. It doesn't really matter where I am. I just pray at that very moment that I am tested. Unfortunately, it happens quite often, but God has really been faithful to me in helping me keep my anger and frustrations from getting out of control.

Patience, dear reader, is definitely a key to harmony in relationships, but before we can turn that key it will help us to understand the meaning of godly patience.

The Meaning of Patience

If you're like me, you probably think of patience as being able to wait a very long time for something. But much more is involved in the kind of patience that is a fruit of the Spirit, as this illustration suggests. Suppose patience were available in a can at the grocery store. What divine ingredients would be written on the label?

Ingredient #1— The first and primary ingredient in patience is *endurance*. This steadfastness of the soul under provocation includes the idea of forbearing wrong and ill-treatment.[2] Patient endurance is long-spiritedness,[3] tolerance, and slowness to wrath.[4] The old King James word "long-suffering" paints the picture of patience pretty clearly for us.

This ingredient of patient endurance is practiced primarily toward people and relates to our attitude toward others.[5] William Barclay points out that "generally speaking the word is not used of patience in regard to things or events but in regard to people."[6] As one scholar succinctly stated, "It is the quality of putting up with other people, even when…sorely tried!"[7]

Ingredient #2— The label describing patience next details the very special conditions for patience: *when injured*. You see, we need patience to endure injuries inflicted by others,[8] a patience that is characterized by long-suffering, evenness of temper, or patient endurance when injured by another.[9] Godly patience also includes the idea of forbearance of wrong under ill-treatment.[10] As one source explains, "Patience is that calm and unruffled temper with which the good [person] bears the evils of life…[that] proceed from [others]."[11] It is when you or I suffer ill treatment inflicted by other people and when we are provoked or wronged that we most need patience. Dr. George Sweeting wrote, "A large part of being kind is the patient willingness to put up with the abuse or ridicule that comes our way. Usually that patience is needed most just when it is exhausted. So often our tolerance level wears thin at the wrong time and our spirit of kindness melts away. Real love…is patient, and it never gives up."[12] Godly patience shines the brightest when pain is inflicted upon us.

Ingredient #3—Another ingredient on the label describing patience is *mercy*. God's patience is always connected with mercy[13] and bears with others for their good.[14] Patience wishes well to others and is willing to endure with them…hoping for their good.

William Barclay shares a sobering insight about mercy when he writes, "If God had been a man, He would have wiped out this world long ago, but He has that patience which bears with all of our sinning and will not cast us off. [Therefore] in our dealings with our fellow men we must reproduce this loving, forbearing, forgiving, patient attitude of God."[15] We are actually acting like God when we are patient with people!

And why does God delay the punishment of man? One day, when I was reviewing a packet of Bible verses I've memorized, I came to a verse about the second coming of the Lord: "The Lord is not slow about His promise [to come again], as some count slowness, but is patient toward you, not wishing for any to perish but *for all to come to repentance*" (2 Peter 3:9, emphasis added). Peter is suggesting here that the Lord is waiting to come again, desiring for more souls to believe and come to salvation. In other words, He is giving mankind an extended opportunity to receive Christ! Behold the patience—and mercy—of God!

This example of God's patience certainly gives you and me a good reason to wait patiently ourselves! Besides obedience to God's instructions to be patient, our motivation to practice patience should be the good of others. We should be consumed with the same thought God has for others: "If I just wait long enough, maybe something good and wonderful will happen to this person!"

Ingredient #4—Finally, written in red letters across the label on our can of patience are these words: "*Contains no anger or vengeance!*" The Spirit's patience holds no wrath or thought of sinful revenge[16] or retaliation.[17] Patience is the grace of the man who *could* revenge himself but *chooses* not to.[18] And, as children of God, we never have any reason to avenge ourselves anyway because God has promised us, "Never take your own revenge… but leave room for the wrath of God, for it is written, 'Vengeance is Mine, I will repay,' says the Lord" (Romans 12:19). As Tertullian, the early church father, observed, "If thou endurest wrong for Christ's sake, he is a revenger"![19]

Therefore, patience withholds: It withholds vengeance, revenge, and retaliation, and endures instead. It endures ill treatment, it refuses to be angry, and it desires the offender's good.

Even very spiritual Christians struggle with this element of patience. Reading in a biography about John Wesley, I was shocked to learn that Mrs. John Wesley is rated as one of the worst wives in all history.[20] Her ugly temperament made life difficult not only for John Wesley, but also for his brother Charles, who had such trouble with his sister-in-law that he said, "I must pray or sink into a spirit of revenge!"[21]

In light of these ingredients, the definition of patience I use for myself is: *Patience does nothing.* Patience is the front end of these three fruit which relate to people—patience, goodness, and kindness—and it is the passive part of love:[22] It is love doing nothing.

As I said, this is the passive end of these three fruit, and we'll move up the "action scale" in the next two chapters. But for now, if you want to walk in patience when you've been hurt, wronged, or ill treated, do nothing! Instead of reacting and doing something outwardly negative and harmful and sinful, inwardly resist in patience. Doing *nothing* gives you and me time (even a second!) to do *something*—to pray, to reflect, and to plan to respond in a righteous manner. So, my dear friend, we must go to God for His patience…and then do nothing that will cause us to lose any of those precious contents. And, just a hint: This process is usually accomplished while kneeling in prayer!

Struggling for Patience

Think about our struggle with patience for a minute: Which is easier—to give in to emotions and anger when someone has hurt you, or to practice patience and hold back your wrath? To lash out with cruel words, or to hold back your hateful words? I know that I have very little problem letting go, losing my temper, and telling my offender exactly how I feel and what I think! But much harder for me is the godly response—God's response!—of choosing to do nothing outwardly as I resist in patience inwardly. Believe me, it takes all of God's strength to help me to do nothing! I desperately need God's Spirit to fill me with His patience. But once you and I are filled, then doing nothing as we resist in patience is how we practice patient endurance...when we're injured by others...without vengeance...and for their good!

Obviously, learning about the ingredients of true spiritual patience can make a drastic difference in our conduct toward others. This knowledge can also help us exhibit the same patience Jesus did in His treatment of others, even His enemies. But to follow in Jesus' footsteps, we'll have to lean heavily on God, because "only by strength imparted by God and by means of complete reliance on the sustaining power of His sovereign, transforming grace will [we] be able to heed [these] directions."[23] How lovely to be a Christian robed in God's patience!

Looking at God's Instructions About Patience

The Bible is an ocean of instruction regarding patience, and I want us to dip into that vast pool and discover several truths about patience, with the help of several examples.

God is patient. In 1 Peter 3:20, we are given an opportunity to marvel at the patience of God. Here we read, "The patience of God kept waiting in the days of Noah, during the construction of the ark." Do you know how long God waited? One hundred

twenty years! Desiring that many would be saved, God waited
120 years before the rain and the flood (Genesis 6:3), making His
salvation available to others. How sad to read that only eight people were in the ark after God waited for so long!

So now we must consider ourselves! How long can you and
I wait? Think of the people in your life, your own loved ones—
maybe a husband who still hasn't believed, or a child who is taking
longer than you wish to yield to God, or a brother or sister whose
unbelief causes your heart to break. God calls us to patience—
His patience. Patience that holds on and won't give up or let go or
cast off the loved one. Patience that continues to extend fresh love
every day—even for 120 years! Certainly this example of God's
patient waiting makes me think I could wait just a little longer!
How about you?

Jesus was patient. Jesus, the Master Teacher, also instructs us
about patience in relationships with problem people, even people He labels as "enemies." Jesus tells us to love our enemies (Luke
6:27) and then explains how to do just that: "Pray…for those
who mistreat you" (verse 28). What a perfect picture of patience
in *action!*

But what is your natural tendency when *you* are insulted or
treated badly? I know that mine is to react and treat the offender
in exactly the same way he or she treated me! But that kind of
response makes my conduct as wrong as my offender's. That is
sin upon sin, creating two wrongs. As Christians you and I are
not to be returning evil for evil, or insult for insult, but to be giving a blessing instead (1 Peter 3:9). Reaction and retaliation are
definitely the fleshly and wrong response. What Jesus wants from
us is the godly response of patience: He wants us to do nothing in fleshly response and instead give a blessing and pray. Isn't
that exactly what Jesus did when He prayed for His killers while
dying on the very cross they had nailed Him to—"Father, forgive

them; for they do not know what they are doing" (Luke 23:34)? Our godly response, dear sister, is prayer—kneeling to pray, being filled with God's patience...and then doing nothing.

This scene from the life of our suffering Savior is too sacred to leave without responding from the depths of our soul! If we really want to be like Jesus, we have to ask ourselves if we're willing to do what we have to do to love our enemies. Do we love Jesus enough to willfully forsake our anger and pride and instead humbly, patiently wait for God to act? Do we love those for whom Jesus died enough to endure patiently with them as He did with us? Do we really love our enemies, those who hate us and curse us and use us? It was Christ's love for such people that put Him on the cross. Therefore, if we desire to love as Jesus loves, then we have to be willing to follow in His steps (1 Peter 2:21) to resist our fleshly urges and instead be patient. Pray now for the Spirit of God to fill you with this sweet fruit.

Paul was patient. Speaking from his own experience, the apostle Paul addressed our behavior towards those who are not Christians. He tells us that we "must not be quarrelsome, but kind to all, able to teach, patient when wronged..." (2 Timothy 2:24). And why would we need to be patient in this case? Verses 25 and 26 answer this question: "with gentleness correcting those who are in opposition, if perhaps God may grant them repentance leading to the knowledge of the truth, and they may come to their senses and escape from the snare of the devil." So, in our encounters with unbelievers, we should practice patience because we are hoping for their salvation.

I thank God that's what my friend Jan did with me! Throughout junior high and high school, Jan was a constant companion and one of my best friends. In fact, we were such good friends that at college we roomed together in the dormitory until Jan moved to one sorority house and I moved to another. Then something wonderful happened to Jan. She became a Christian, and she wanted to tell me, a best friend, all about it!

So one evening after dinner Jan came to share her good news and invite me to attend her Bible study. I wish I could tell you I was sweet and behaved like a lady. Even more than that, I wish I could tell you I went with her to her meeting and embraced Christ as well. But no, I was so shocked that all I could do was ridicule her and laugh at her. Basically, I told Jan, "Prove it!" I wanted to see some big changes in her life before I was going to believe what she was telling me.

Well, through the years, Jan was faithful to grow in Christ. And she was a faithful friend to me. She kept reaching out to me, never giving up on me. I, however, gave up on her. Ten years passed, years of lost friendship as I allowed my lack of under-standing to drive a wedge between us. Jan and I hadn't talked for a decade when, in another state halfway across the nation, I sud-denly and dramatically became a Christian! And guess what? I wanted to call Jan immediately. I wanted to tell her about my experience…and I wanted to ask her forgiveness for mistreating her. Today I'm glad to say that we correspond and share in the things of the Lord. Jan lived out for me patience with an unbe-liever, and because she desired the best for me, she remained faith-ful as a friend—even while being mistreated!

Sarah was not patient. Sometimes we learn just as much from negative examples as positive ones! And for us the Old Testament princess Sarah shows us a picture of a lack of patience. As Sarah and her husband Abraham followed God, they had the special privilege of hearing many of God's promises from God Himself. One of those promises was an heir for them…yet there was no child until Sarah was ninety years old and Abraham was ninety-nine. And Sarah did not handle the wait well at all!

Because her continued barrenness brought her such constant

grief, Sarah became "the woman who made a great mistake."[24] Her impatience led her to propose the following plan to Abraham: Go in to my maid Hagar and conceive a child (Genesis 16:2). Although the custom of that time allowed for a man with a barren wife to take a concubine in order to have an heir,[25] this mistake produced not only historical tragedy but fierce jealousy and contention between Sarah and Hagar.

And pregnancy brought out the worst in Hagar. When she saw that she had conceived, she despised Sarah (Genesis 16:4). Hagar became insolent and rebellious, acting in pride and contempt toward Sarah. This is how Hagar became the ever-present problem-person in childless Sarah's life!

How did Sarah handle this people-problem, this daily dilemma? Certainly not the way we would hope! In an ugly scene marked by Hagar's pride and disdain toward her mistress and Sarah's envy of her pregnant slave, Sarah treated Hagar so harshly that she fled from Sarah's presence (16:6). Sarah lost her patience and persecuted her servant. Although Sarah did grow to exhibit great faith (Hebrews 11:11), here she lashed out at Hagar—probably physically as well as verbally. At this point, she is an example of a woman who lacked patience. She acted out hatred, strife, jealousy, wrath, faction, sedition, and envy—many of the works of the flesh which Paul lists in Galatians 5:19-21. No, this is *not* a pretty picture!

As I think about Sarah, a woman exalted for her faith, I ask myself, "Isn't faith what lies beneath our patience?" And the answer is yes—which takes us right back to love and joy and peace. These three fruit of the Spirit grow out of our relationship with God and the realization that He is the Author and Designer of our life and of all that enters it—even childlessness, even a Hagar. So, my friend, whenever we feel impatient, we must look again into the face of God, acknowledge Him, His wisdom, His ways, and His choices for our life, exhale…and do nothing, as we resist in patience. This is the kind of faith that makes patience grow...and makes us women who walk with God.

Hannah was patient. Very much like Sarah, Hannah, too, was on the receiving end of daily persecution and provocation. As we learned back in chapter 4, Hannah's adversary was Peninnah, her husband's other wife and a rival who provoked her bitterly year after year (1 Samuel 1:6-7). Yet Hannah was patient. And we can be sure she had all of the same thoughts, feelings, and urges that Sarah had! But Hannah handled these emotions in a godly way: She went to the temple of the Lord and prayed to Him, speaking to Him about her persecution and her pain (verses 10-16).

Yes, Hannah gives us a godly model for enduring ill treatment. We are not to fight back or lose our control. Instead, we are to run to God, hide ourselves in Him, and adorn ourselves with His cloak of patience! Only God can help us do nothing and resist in patience. It's a struggle, but you and I must constrain our natural, fleshly urges to do combat and instead draw from God's fathomless fountain all the patience we need. Then the Holy Spirit will display the glory of His patience, enabling us to successfully do nothing.

Waiting for the Judge

One evening while I was teaching on this fruit of the Spirit, I talked to my class about how to grow in God's patience. In short, I told my students to remember to *wait for the judge.* Let me explain.

In an encouraging passage written to a group of poor and oppressed Christians, the apostle James appeals to these saints to "be patient...until the coming of the Lord" (James 5:7). He tells them to "be patient...for the coming of the Lord is at hand" (verse 8). Then he says, "Behold, the judge is standing right at the door" (verse 9). Three times James speaks of the coming of the

Lord and the fact that He is at hand, indeed standing right at the door. But exactly how was this information supposed to encourage these bewildered saints—and us as well?

First of all, the promise of our Lord's return brings great hope to our sore hearts, for when He does arrive, things will change (Revelation 21:3-4)! Oppression will come to an end: Our suffering at the hands of others will be over. We will also enjoy the continuing presence of Jesus. Not only that, but the Lord will reward us for the obedience we've exhibited throughout our life (Revelation 22:12). He will also take vengeance upon our enemies, judging appropriately and correcting abuses. Indeed, *everything* will be made right as Christ, the Judge, brings justice and vindicates the righteous!

I know that this image of a judge makes James's call for patience easier for me to accept and apply. It's the picture of an Old Testament circuit-rider judge like Samuel, who annually traveled his circuit, judging the affairs of the people (1 Samuel 7:16).[26] The one problem with that set-up was that people had to *wait* until Samuel showed up in their town to settle matters among themselves. And, in the meantime, possibly up to a year, they had to exist together with disputes and injustices. They had to wait patiently and do nothing...until the judge came and made everything right.

It's a tall order, but like those waiting people, you and I are to exist together with unsettled disputes and injustices until our Lord, the Judge, arrives to settle things. We are to continue to live with our adversaries and endure ill treatment from difficult people, all the while remaining patient and practicing self-restraint. We are not to turn to self-pity or complaining (see James 5:7-9). And we are not to judge, quarrel, criticize, gossip, or find fault. No, we are responsible for only one thing while we wait, and that is Christlike conduct. The Judge is responsible for everything else!

And so, dear one, with this image in mind, ask yourself, "Can

I wait?" James says you can. Therefore pick the person in your life who has caused you the most personal pain—longstanding pain or pain that's related to what's happening in your life right now. Before the Lord—the Judge—select the person who is hostile, mean, or ungrateful, who ignores you, insults you, slanders you, or blocks your progress. Then—through prayer and by God's grace and His help—resist every urge to retaliate or punish that person and instead do nothing. In patience, do nothing while you wait for the Judge.

Things to Do Today to Walk in Patience

God's Word is faithful to come to our rescue as we seek to walk with Him in the trying area of patience. What does the Bible suggest you and I can do?

- Train yourself in long-suffering. Proverbs 19:11 offers this wisdom: "A man's [or woman's] discretion makes him slow to anger, and it is his glory to overlook a transgression." In other words, learn to restrain your anger.

- Lengthen your fuse. How long can you wait? Well, make that period a little longer. How many times can you wait? Make it a few more times next time. That's where prayer comes into play. Our patient God is willing to give you His patience whenever you ask.

- Remove opportunities to sin. As Paul says, "Make no provision for the flesh" (Romans 13:14). And Proverbs instructs us that "keeping away from strife is an honor for a man, but any fool will quarrel" (20:3).

- Follow Jesus' example. No one has ever endured more abuse than Jesus did! Yet He remained absolutely sinless even under the most severe mistreatment: "He committed no sin, nor was any deceit found in His mouth; and while

being reviled, He did not revile in return; while suffering, He uttered no threats" (1 Peter 2:22-23). Carry Jesus' response to suffering in your heart and mind…and try to lift your own responses to a higher level of godliness.

- Pray. This was Jesus' sure-fire method for enduring His suffering: He just "kept entrusting Himself to Him who judges righteously" (1 Peter 2:23). So, precious one, when you are injured by others, turn your aching soul heavenward. Allow God to soothe your pain as you do nothing. Let Him fill you with His patience as you endure the hurt, without vengeance and for the good of those who hurt you. After all, it was by Jesus' wounds that you and I were healed (verse 24). It was for our good that He suffered. And we are called to do the same—to be patient with others for their own good. There is no higher privilege for us as Christians.

7

Planning for Kindness

⁓⁂⁓

The fruit of the Spirit is…kindness.
GALATIANS 5:22

As we rang the door bell, neither of us imagined what was waiting on the other side of that door! My friend Judy and I had driven for 45 minutes through the outlying hills of the San Fernando Valley to the home of another friend who was hostessing a bridal shower. Yet the door was opened by someone else…who explained that our hostess's father had passed away just thirty minutes earlier and that she had left for the hospital.

Stunned, the three of us huddled to pray for our friend and all that she was facing at that moment. But after the action of prayer, it was time for us to go into action ourselves in the kitchen! As the many guests began to arrive, Judy and I offered emergency help. When brunch was served, I worked kitchen duty while Judy moved among the women asking if they needed anything, patting them on the shoulder, and making sure everyone was comfortable. Graciously Judy chatted with each woman as she carried the heavy silver coffeepot around the room, refilling cups and removing dirty dishes and soiled napkins. Then even I, in the kitchen, could hear one guest sneer as Judy moved out of ear-shot, "She's too nice."

Beloved, since that morning, I've given much thought to those words, "She's too nice." What Judy did for all of us—including an ungrateful woman—was actively live out kindness, the next fruit of the Spirit. Judy modeled the grace and ministry of kind-ness not only for those other women, but for me as well. As you'll soon see, the highest compliment a Christian woman can receive is to be described as "too nice." When people say that of you or me, we can know we are truly exhibiting the Spirit's fruit!

Our Calling to Kindness

But…back to our walk with God! In this section of our book we're learning about the *actions* of patience, kindness, and good-ness in dealing with the people in our life. As we face people each day and experience any pain they may inflict upon us, we are to be patient and be careful not to do anything sinful or harm-ful when provoked. This godly response is achieved when we ask God to fill us with His patience. Only He can help us to do nothing! But, having asked for patience, it is now time to make a move, to go into action, to get up and do something. And that "something" is kindness, the next fruit on the Lord's list; "the fruit of the Spirit is…kindness" (Galatians 5:22).

Just as our Lord is kind, we as His women are called to be kind, too. And, even though the fruit of kindness is borne in our lives as we walk by the Spirit, that walk involves living out sev-eral commands given to us in God's Word. One of these com-mands follows on the heels of a passage of Scripture (Ephesians 4:25-32) which scholar William Barclay entitles "Things Which Must Be Banished from Life."[1] In these verses, the apostle Paul warns Christians against conduct that grieves the Holy Spirit and hurts the heart of God.[2] This conduct includes various forms of meanness (bitterness, wrath, anger, clamor, and evil speaking), all of which God calls us to banish from our lives. Instead, we are to "be kind to one another" (verse 32). The Living Bible says straightforwardly: "Stop being mean…[and] instead, be kind to each other." It's obvious that our kindness is indeed an action that pleases God!

Another call to kindness is sounded forth in Colossians 3:12. Here God tells us to "put on a heart of…kindness." Kindness is one of the basic Christian virtues that helps govern human relationships. Therefore you and I are to put on kindness in all our relationships. How exquisite to have kindness characterize our life and actions!

God issues one more call to kindness in 2 Timothy 2:24. Here the apostle Paul tells us how to act toward those who are not Christians: "The Lord's bond-servant must not be quarrelsome, but be kind to all." It's a fact that kindness has been an important element in Christian witnessing since the early centuries. As one missionary reports, Christians have been known through the ages by their love and concern for others, and some of the most telling evidence of this comes not from the mouths of Christians themselves but from the critics of Christianity who were concerned that Christianity was specially advanced through their loving service rendered to strangers.[3]

And now, dear Christian, we must pause a moment and reflect upon God's charges to us to be kind. Do you consider yourself to be kind? Are you trying to "stop being mean" and to instead put on a heart of compassion and kindness toward others? Are you seeking to please God by your kindness rather than cause the Holy Spirit sorrow by any unkindness? As you spiritually prepare yourself each morning, do you choose to put on the robe of kindness? For us to walk with God means we must walk in the way of kindness.

Defining Kindness

Having acknowledged our calling to be kind, our next concern is to better understand it. It helps to know that kindness has been defined as tenderness[4] and concern for other people.[5] It is the virtue of the person whose neighbor's good is as dear to him as his own.[6] Kindness is also a sweetness of disposition[7] and a matter of the heart. Certainly God's grace of kindness should pervade the whole person, mellowing all that might be harsh.[8]

My own definition of kindness—which helps me immensely in cultivating and practicing this spirit of concern for others—is *kindness plans to do something*. While patience means doing nothing sinful while resisting in patience (see chapter 6), kindness now plans to act. Kindness, like all the other fruit of the Spirit, desires godly action and therefore plans for those actions. First we were filled with God's patience: We knelt humbly in prayer to keep from losing a drop of it by doing something rash or reactive. Now, acting out of love and filled with God's kindness as well as His patience, we get up and go looking for opportunities to do something. Do you remember that patience is the passive end of love (doing nothing when provoked)? Well, now we see kindness actively move out, preparing for the action of goodness (which we will look at in the next chapter). Kindness goes out looking, wondering, and asking, "Who needs love? How can I ease someone's burden? How can I touch another person?"

Learning from Opposites

We can learn even more about kindness when we look at its opposites. For instance, arguing. Certain behaviors signal to us that we are not walking by the Spirit or practicing God's kindness, and one of those flashing red lights is arguing. In 2 Timothy 2:24, Paul says that the Lord's bond-servant must not be quarrelsome, but be *kind* to all. Therefore, when you or I find ourselves striving or quarrelling, arguing or quibbling, we can be sure that this behavior "is not that which comes down from above" (James 3:15), but is instead coming from our own flesh. Galatians 5:20 even lists strife, disputing, and dissension among the evil deeds of the flesh.

Imagine the home...the office...or the church without any arguing! And imagine the same energy that contention, strife, and arguing consume channeled toward kindness instead. Exactly what would you and I have to do to help make that happen? Here's a short list.

- Love others more than ourselves.

- Care for the comfort and welfare of others more than our own.

- Consider others more important than ourselves (Philippians 2:3).

- Forego quarrelling.

Matthew 11:28-30 helps us gain even greater insight into kindness from another pair of opposites. Speaking words of comfort to His followers, Jesus issues a gentle invitation: "Come unto Me, all who are weary and heavy-laden, and I will give you rest. Take My yoke upon you, and learn from Me, for I am gentle and humble in heart; and you shall find rest for your souls. For My yoke is easy [that is, kind], and My load is light." It's helpful for us to understand that a yoke was a wooden frame placed upon a person's shoulders that was meant to make his load easier to carry. However, if the load was unequally distributed or simply too heavy, that yoke would begin to chafe and rub and wear the person down. Here Jesus is contrasting His yoke and the burden He asks His followers to bear with the yoke of trying to keep all of the rules laid upon the Jews by Israel's teachers, and He says that His yoke is "easy"—which is the same word as "kind." In fact, one scholar translates the verse "My yoke is kindly."[9]

I have to admit that the vividness of this mental image caused me to ask some hard questions about my relationships with others—and maybe you would like to do the same. For instance, what is it like to be yoked with me at home, on a committee, in a project, or in a ministry? Am I an asset to those around me, a person who doesn't chafe? Am I easy to be with and kind, a person who makes it easier for other people to bear their burdens? Or am I an additional burden which others must bear, causing their yoke to chafe and rub, making it more difficult for them to pull their weight because they are yoked to a harsh, quarrelsome, wearisome woman? Do my manner and lack of kindness chafe, rub, and wear others down? Kindness means making life easier for others—not harder—just as Jesus makes your life and mine easier.

Cultivating Kindness

The book I turn to each morning during prayer time contains a sobering prompt that has helped me grow in kindness (and I hope it helps you, too). Every week, I read a prompt that instructs me to pray for "greater love and compassion for others." Well, I have to tell you that whenever I see these words, I am humbled to the core as I examine my heart and soul. This call to prayer always makes me realize how much more I need this godly quality in my life! But prayer and the following aspects of kindness have helped me to cultivate the fruit of kindness. These thoughts have given me a handle on what kindness does—and they can do the same for you.

1. *Caring is a part of kindness.* It's true that when we genuinely care about someone, we find ourselves paying attention to the circumstances of their lives and being concerned about their welfare. We get involved in their lives. As our love grows for another person, the details of that person's life become more and more

important to us. It begins to matter greatly to us if they are sad or discouraged, struggling or in pain, needy or lonely. But I know for myself that such concern doesn't come nearly as easily for the problem people in my life!

I've found prayer to be one sure way to nurture care for those who bring me pain. It's true that if you and I will follow Jesus' instruction to "pray for those who mistreat you" (Luke 6:28), startling changes will occur in our heart. For starters, the bond of prayer causes us to become vitally and spiritually involved in the lives of the individuals we pray for. Also, through prayer, God changes *our* heart and mind by softening our harshness and melting our selfishness into concern for others—including our enemies!

Another act that makes a marked difference in our relationships is a decision to care for others—as one college teacher knew when she gave an unusual assignment to her seniors. She said, "Select the person on campus you dislike the most. Daily during the coming month go out of your way to do some act of kindness for that person." Later one student reported, "By the end of the month my dislike of [the woman selected] had been replaced by a growing compassion and understanding.... [This assignment] helped me see things about myself—my unfriendliness, my lack of compassion, my judging without first trying to understand the causes of behavior I disliked."[10] It's no surprise that caring about others truly dispels unfriendliness, a lack of compassion, and a judgmental spirit. So...ask God to help you (as my prayer guide suggests) have greater love and compassion for others.

2. *Thinking is a part of kindness.* Another sure sign that we are growing in our concern for people is when we begin to think about others and the conditions of their lives. We'll find ourselves looking at people and thinking, "What would help her? What would help him? What does he need? What does she need?" We'll

find ourselves asking God, "How can I serve this person? How can I make his or her life easier? How can I touch their life, lift their burden?" As we are learning, kindness plans to do something, and that takes a certain amount of thought and prayer before the Lord—as David models for us. When he became the king of Israel, David asked, "Is there yet anyone left of the house of Saul [the previous king], that I may show him kindness…?" (2 Samuel 9:1). You see, David was *thinking* about showing kindness to the heirs of the former king. Can you think of someone you can be kind to?

There's no doubt that the greatest training ground for thinking about the welfare of others is right in our own home. My friend Ann has thought of dozens of ways to show kindness to her family. One way involves a beautiful red plate which has in gold lettering the words, "You are very special!" A part of her joy as a wife and mother is showing simple kindnesses to a discouraged family member—such as setting that person's place at the table with her special red plate!

So, precious sister, ask God to give you a caring heart and a creative mind as you, too, begin looking around to see the needs of people in your home, your neighborhood, your work place, and your church. Hurting people are literally everywhere! One staggering statistic reports, "Ninety percent of all mental illness… could have been prevented, or could yet be cured, by simple kindness."[11] What can you think of doing today that would touch another life with kindness?

3. *Noticing is a part of kindness.* Still another way to practice kindness is to notice other people's needs. All we have to do is use our God-given capacity for observation: As the Bible says, "The hearing ear and the seeing eye, the Lord has made both of them" (Proverbs 20:12). We can *always* be watching and listening to those around us. In fact, this is one of the ways God cares for us:

"The eyes of the Lord are upon the righteous, and His ears attend to their prayer" (1 Peter 3:12). And you and I can care for people in the same way God cares for us…just by paying attention and being on the lookout for people's needs.

I read of an evangelist's mother who practiced such kindness and observation: "One day he found her sitting at the table with an old tramp. Apparently she had gone shopping, met the tramp along the way, and invited him home for a warm meal. During the conversation the tramp said, 'I wish there were more people like you in the world.' Whereupon his mother replied, 'Oh, there are! But you must just look for them.' The old man simply shook his head saying, 'But lady, I didn't need to look for you. You looked for me!'"[12] When you or I begin to notice others, we'll soon know their wants and needs just as this kind and godly woman did. The Bible gives us examples of kindness as well— examples that can help you in your walk with God.

In the Old Testament, *the Shunammite woman* was a person who noticed. She noticed the prophet Elisha frequently passing by her home with no apparent place to lodge or eat (2 Kings 4:8-10). Well, kindness went into action as she persuaded him to eat food. "And so it was, as often as he passed by, he turned in there to eat food" (verse 8).

As she cared and thought and noticed, she soon realized that he had no other place to stay. Acting again on her concern, she asked her husband, "Please, let us make a little walled upper chamber and let us set a bed for him there, and a table and a chair and a lampstand; and it shall be, when he comes to us, that he can turn in there" (verse 10). This woman's eyes were open, and so was her heart and her home. In her kindness, she noticed Elisha's needs.

Another woman of the Bible who noticed people's needs was *Dorcas*. God describes her as a woman "abounding with deeds of kindness and charity, which she continually did" (Acts 9:36).

Among her kind deeds was sewing tunics and garments for the widows (verse 39). What had Dorcas seen with her eyes and heard with her ears? She had noticed that the widows needed clothes—and she acted.

Of course *Jesus*, "the kindness of God" in flesh (Titus 3:4), always noticed the needs of the people around Him. In the Gospels we're told how He was moved with compassion when He looked upon the hungry multitude. He knew their needs and wanted to give them something to eat (Luke 9:13). His heart of kindness was also a rebuke to His disciples, who wanted to send the multitude away (verse 12). While Jesus cared and was concerned, the Twelve scorned the people and their needs. While Jesus was moved with compassion, they saw the people as bothersome. O for the grace to be like Jesus!

There's a story Anne Ortlund shares in her book *Disciplines of the Beautiful Woman* that shows us a woman who walks in kindness. Mrs. Ortlund writes of "a Hawaiian woman who strings a number of leis early each Sunday morning, not for anyone in particular! Then she goes to church praying, 'Lord, who needs my leis today? A newcomer? Someone discouraged. Lead me to the right people.'"[13] Yes, this is clearly a picture of kindness—a person filled with God's love going out looking; kindness planning to do something; kindness keeping a keen eye out and noticing others; kindness actively seeking those who are in need. May you and I follow in her kind footsteps!

4. *Touching is a part of kindness.* It helps us to cultivate kindness when we think of kindness as the tender touch of concern and compassion. At the bridal shower I told you about earlier, Judy's gestures of kindness included touching the women as she served them and cared for them. The same should be true of us. When we minister to others in gentle kindness, touch is something we almost instinctively give to those we care about. We

can be like the apostle Paul who wrote that he was gentle among the Thessalonians "as a nursing mother tenderly cares for her own children" (1 Thessalonians 2:7). Indeed, a mother's care for a nursing infant is an image of pure and gentle tenderness!

Our Savior also demonstrated perfect kindness when He held little children. When eager parents brought their children to Him so that He might touch them, the disciples rebuked them (Mark 10:13). I can imagine them hissing, "Shoo! Get these kids out of here! Don't bother the Master. This is kingdom work!" But, after rebuking His disciples for their lack of kindness, Jesus took those little children into His arms and blessed them, laying His hands upon them (verse 16).

Yes, our Jesus was kind and tender, and He always touched the people He was caring for. He stopped and touched the coffin of a widow's only son (Luke 7:12-15). He touched the deformed, bent-over back of a suffering woman (Luke 13:10-13). He stretched out His hand and touched a man "full of leprosy" (Luke 5:12-13). He touched the two blind men's eyes (Matthew 20:29-34). The Law forbade each of these acts of touching, acts which made a man unclean and unfit to worship. Yet in each case Jesus gave His touch—and a miracle followed. The moment He touched the sufferers, they were healed, they were clean, and Jesus therefore maintained His purity in the eyes of the Law.

Aren't you glad that you and I can grow in God's grace of kindness? We can constantly ask God to work in our heart to help us care, think, notice, and touch the people He places in our life. And as we stifle and renounce our unkind emotions and thoughts about others and obey God's command for kindness from us, we can then—by the power of the Holy Spirit—practice kindness.

Becoming "Too Nice"

And now, dear one, it's time for you and me to set out on the path of becoming "too nice." In our culture today, this may

not sound very appealing, but being "too nice" is exactly what
kindness is. When the book of Galatians was written, the common slave-name *chrestos* came from the same Greek root word for
kindness. The first-century pagans, who confused this familiar
name with the unfamiliar *Christos* for Christ, began calling Christians by a nickname that meant "goody-goody"[14]—the same as
being "too nice." The spelling of the two words varies by just one
letter, but what an appropriate similarity! We who walk with God
are indeed to be kind—to be "too nice."

My friend Judy was said to be "too nice." Why? Because she
was kind, because she was serving as a "chrestos," because she
was caring, thinking, noticing, and touching, and because she is
a "Christos," a kind of Christ, a "goody-goody." Judy's kindness
should be a goal for each of us as we continue to grow in this fruit
of the Spirit. As one Bible teacher exhorted, "We need to cultivate resourcefulness in kindliness, to gain proficiency in the artistry of applying Christian love to the hearts and lives of those
with whom we come in contact in the many activities and relationships of life."[15] But what are some things we could do to cultivate this artistry? I have a few thoughts.

Things to Do Today to Walk in Kindness

I've pointed out earlier that this second trio of the fruit of the
Spirit—patience, kindness, and goodness—has to do with our
treatment of others. The order of this listing implies that kindness is the next step we are to take after we have practiced patience
when wronged. I know my natural response when someone has
hurt me is to react and decide, "Well, you're off my list! I don't
have to put up with that kind of treatment! I'll just withhold my
love from you." But as we've been learning, moments like these
are precisely when you and I need to have spiritual victory and be
kind instead. This supernatural act requires God, the Holy Spirit,
filling us with *His* kindness.

So, as you've done before, I'm asking you to choose your number one problem person and take him or her before the Lord in prayer. I also want you to take before God your pain, your harsh thoughts, your temptations to respond in an unchristian manner, and your confessions of times when you've given in to those thoughts or temptations. Acknowledge your unkindness as well as any times when you withheld kindness. Then go a step further and ask God to help you show His kindness to the very person who hurt you, who caused your pain, who is causing you to suffer, and who is making your life miserable. While you are suffering long and waiting patiently under ill-treatment, be kind. For love suffers patiently *and* is kind (1 Corinthians 13:4).

My friend Karen gave me a little calendar so that each day I can flip a page over and read another encouraging statement. Well, one day I learned a little more about kindness as the calendar page read, "Kindness is the ability to love people more than they deserve." Can we do that, dear friend? God says we can—and His Spirit helps us. So...

- Pray for your enemies, those people who mistreat and use you (Luke 6:28). You will find you cannot hate a person you are praying for. You also can't neglect that person. Try it! You'll find these statements to be true because prayer and hatred don't go together. Neither do prayer and neglect.

- Spend time with God owning up to any ill will you have toward an individual or group of people. Ask for God's help in demonstrating the Spirit's kindness to those people.

- Ask God to help you become known more as a comforter and less as a confronter.

- Study Jesus' life for more examples of kindness and then follow in His steps. Keep a journal of those instances of His

kindness as you discover them, noting the circumstances
surrounding His graciousness.

• Begin making the effort at home to live out God's command to be kind to others (Ephesians 4:32). What does
your husband need? Your children? Or your roommates?
What would make their life easier?

• Pray for God to fill your heart with His compassion as you
walk each day and every step along the way with Him.

8

Giving in Goodness

✦

The fruit of the Spirit is...goodness.
GALATIANS 5:22

Late one evening I crawled into bed clutching a book, hoping I could fulfill my nightly goal of reading at least five minutes before turning out the lamp. It had been another wild and full day and I had just about had it...but I was going to give the five minutes a try anyway. The book in my hand was a treasure I had found that morning at the bookstore, and all day long I had been relishing the thought of opening this small delight. There had been only one copy on the shelf at the store, and its title had caught my eye and piqued my curiosity: *People Whose Faith Got Them into Trouble*.[1] Finally it was time—if I could just stay awake! As I began reading this book, subtitled "Stories of Costly Discipleship," the opening words of the first chapter caught my attention so completely that I read much longer than usual. Here's what I read:

The sound of hooves at midnight—horsemen galloping into the courtyard—and the clatter of armor as soldiers surround the house wake the old man.

Two officers dismount and pound on the wooden door with the butt ends of their spears.

Maids in disheveled nightclothes rush upstairs and urge the white-haired fugitive to hide under the bed, in a closet...anywhere. Instead, he hushes them, drapes a cloak over his frail shoulders, descends the stairs, opens the door and invites the men who have come to arrest him inside.

He instructs the maids, "Quickly, prepare hot food and something to drink. Can't you see these men have ridden hard tonight? They need refreshment; give them the best in the house."

Confused by this unexpected reception, the arresting officers crowd into the room and cluster around a bronze charcoal brazier on the floor.

As they warm their numb hands against the cold night of February 22, 166, Polycarp, elderly bishop of Smyrna...makes every effort to see that his guests are comfortable. He personally serves the officers and soldiers alike from the warm dishes his maids have prepared.[2]

What a powerful example of Christian goodness! A man being hunted down, a man who would soon taste death by execution at a fiery stake, was showing love to his persecutors! This man was exhibiting the Spirit's fruit: *Patience* allowed him to graciously receive his captors, *kindness* thought of their needs, and then *goodness* followed through. Serving them himself, the man being led to death met the needs of those leading him. This story of Polycarp offers us a vivid example of the fruit of the Spirit in action.

Reviewing Our Progress

So far in this section of this book, you and I have examined two of the graces that help us in our relationships with people. The first is *patience*. Patience is like a seed hidden beneath the surface, germinating there, quietly and slowly incubating life. Patience silently waits in the dark earth, hidden from view, doing nothing (it seems!). This sweet fruit of patience makes it possible for kindness and goodness to develop.

Next is *kindness*. Kindness grows from the seed of patience in the dark depths of private times with God. Sprouting tiny root hairs that soon develop into a complete root system and the recognizable part of a stem, kindness pushes its head higher and higher toward heaven, stretching itself toward God, wanting to break forth and do something. At last the desires of kindness are fully formed, and the energy of a heart filled with God's kindness enables the plant to crack through the soil.

And now we behold *goodness* pushing its head through the hard, crusted soil...of our heart, of men's hearts, of the evil in the world...and blossoming into works. As we marvel at this fruit—so often sown by the pain and injuries we've suffered at the hands of other people—we can only pause and praise our Father in heaven for His wisdom in knowing how to produce loveliness in our lives, how to bring beauty from ashes (Isaiah 61:3 KJV), how to overcome evil with good (Romans 12:21), and how to transform great sorrow into greater blessing.

Beloved, only our gracious God knows how to grow us to be like Him! Just as a garden is laid out by a plan, God designs your life and mine according to a plan. He uses the people, events, and circumstances of our life to guide us along the path toward godliness, and He leads us step by step. Walking with Him—listening to His voice, humbling ourselves in prayer, following His ways, and imitating His dear Son—we show forth His glory as we bear His fruit. By studying these fruits, we've learned about God's desire for us and for our walk with Him: He wants us to be like Him. And one way to be like Him is to bear His fruit of goodness.

Getting a Handle on Goodness

Bearing the fruit of goodness will be easier if we understand three aspects of the biblical definition of spiritual goodness, aspects which relate to our conduct toward others.

1. *True goodness is spiritual in its origin.* The Bible reveals to us that God is good (Psalm 33:5; Nehemiah 9:25,35). Indeed, from cover to cover, the Bible tells the story of God's gracious goodness! One scholar defines this goodness as "the sum of all God's attributes...express[ing] the...excellence of the divine character."[3] And yet, as God's children, we can exhibit His goodness, a goodness that is so completely upright that it abhors evil.[4] What a blessed privilege to represent Him!

The Bible also shows us that God's goodness is the opposite of *man's badness.*[5] And our badness (as I mentioned in the first chapter) is why we need spiritual help from God. First, *our sin* makes human goodness impossible. As Paul writes in the Book of Romans, "There is none righteous, not even one...there is none who does good, there is not even one" (Romans 3:10,12). And second, we need God's help because of *our flesh.* The apostle Paul accurately expresses for us the struggle that exists in every human—the war with the flesh—when he cries out in despair, "For I know that nothing good dwells in me, that is, in my flesh" (Romans 7:18).

So, due to our sin and our flesh, we need God's grace and the

Spirit's power to exhibit His fruit of goodness, because any and all goodness—genuine goodness—must have God in the formula.

2. *Goodness is active.* As we learned in the preceding chapter, kindness means planning to do something good for others. And now goodness moves into total action. God *in* us and His presence *with* us produces *His* goodness in us. And His goodness in us then results in active benevolence,[6] kindly activity on the behalf of others.[7] I can't think of anything that would glorify God more! Can you?

3. *Goodness is a readiness to do good.* In addition to being active, goodness is completely dedicated to helping others live well.[8] It is a quality that is ruled by and aims at what is good[9]—a readiness to do good.[10] Indeed, goodness is up on tip-toe, ready and waiting to do good.

Don't you agree that our world, our churches, and our homes need people who are actively kind; people who walk out their door every day ready to do good—not just think about it or pray about it; people who are devoted to making the lives of others better? Trying to define goodness, it helps me to understand it as *goodness does everything!* Goodness will do everything it can to shower God's goodness upon others. Goodness follows through on those wonderful thoughts of kindness, thoughts which came when we were praying, caring, noticing, and planning to act. Goodness takes the step from good intentions to actively serving others. John Wesley understood this principle and made it his rule for life...and we should, too:

> Do all the good you can,
> by all the means you can,
> in all the ways you can,
> in all the places you can,
> at all the times you can,

to all the people you can,
as long as ever you can.

Getting a Handle on Walking in Goodness

Now let me show you how God's goodness in us works itself out. The presence of the Holy Spirit within us should make a difference in the way we live and how we treat others. That's why God calls us to "walk in newness of life" (Romans 6:4); "walk in a manner worthy of the calling with which you have been called" (Ephesians 4:1); "walk in love" (Ephesians 5:2); "walk as children of light" (Ephesians 5:8); "walk in Him" (Colossians 2:6); "walk in a manner worthy of the God who calls you" (1 Thessalonians 2:12); "walk in the same manner as [Jesus] walked" (1 John 2:6); and "walk by the Spirit" (Galatians 5:16).

Walking with God (which is what this book is all about) requires that you and I make serious choices. As one fellow traveler notes, "The Spirit life includes goodness, and goodness doesn't come naturally; it always requires a decision."[11] And our relationships with others, especially with those who hurt us—the arena where we live out patience, kindness, and goodness—call for choices, too. One definite choice we can make when we're hurt by someone is to walk in *patience* and *do nothing*. Then, having made this choice (*not* to blow up, *not* to tell someone off, *not* to succumb to anger, *not* to fight back, *not* to retaliate), we can move to the next choice—the choice of *kindness*—and *plan to do something*, plan to do deeds of kindness.

Do you see how God's grace released in us as we walk by the Spirit produces miracle after miracle in our lives? For instance, Miracle #1: Instead of an outburst of anger or hatred, love in the form of patience is lived out. Then Miracle #2: Our heart changes from the *natural* desire for revenge to the *supernatural* desire for the good of others. Goodness prays, "What can I do to love this person for Christ's sake?" And now Miracle #3: Goodness does everything! Goodness puts God's love into actions, follows through on our plans for kindness, and gives—indeed, pours out!—God's love to others.

Oh, dear reader, *this* kind of living—characterized by God's patience, kindness, and goodness—*is* walking by the Spirit! *This* kind of living overcomes evil with good (Romans 12:21), does not return evil for evil or insult for insult, but gives a blessing instead (1 Peter 3:9). *This* kind of living is spiritual victory—victory of the Spirit over the flesh—and evidence of God at work in our life. And *this* kind of living is godly living because only God in us can do this!

We must always remember that the fruit is His. As we practice obedience to God's commands, He produces His fruit in us. And it is also produced by His grace and glorifies him: We are told to let our light shine before men in such a way that they may see our good works, and glorify our Father who is in heaven (Matthew 5:16). However, the choice to do as Romans 6:13 tells us, to yield ourselves unto God and our members as instruments of righteousness unto God and not unto sin is ours.

This choice, my friend, is the focus of our constant battle between the flesh and the Spirit (Galatians 5:17). You and I must put forth the effort of making the right choices—God's choices. And we must turn to God for His help in gaining victory over sin. Then, miracle of miracles, our life will indeed bring glory to Him as His fruit grows and displays itself in our walk with Him!

Choosing Goodness

Some of the women in my evening Bible class were sobered by the choices they had to make on their walk with God. Susan, for instance, was hurt by neighbors who are not Christians and who openly despise her for being one. She told me her plan of action: "I set a goal. No matter what they do or say in passing, I decided

I'm going to respond in goodness—and I insist that my children do the same. We are to be Christ's examples. And it's already working! The mother has started smiling and saying hello, and I'm hoping that the father will follow soon."

Ann, too, was hurt—but by the Christian women in her Bible study. What did she do? How did she handle this? How did she respond? "I chose not to feel hurt about not being invited to join them on their outing. I chose to not feel bitterness or resentment. I just need to show my love for them."

And then there is Maria, who daily faces a hostile, persecuting boss, a person she describes as rude and abrasive. Her situation at work boiled down to a spiritual decision for her: She could react in an ungodly way or respond in godliness. She wrote, "I had to make a choice—give back what he is dishing out or show him the kindness and goodness of the Lord."

Examples like these go on and on and the choices like these go on and on, but I'm sure you get a picture of how to walk in goodness from these few glimpses. Like these wonderful women, our walk with God requires many decisions on our part as we constantly look to God, asking Him, "What is the right thing to do?"

Recognizing Goodness as an Assignment from God

Any time I've held down a job, I've always had a written job assignment. And, because the responsibilities were in writing, I always knew what was expected of me. Any time I was unsure, all I had to do was get out that description, read it again, and find direction for my efforts. Well, my friend, as believers you and I have a written job assignment, too. God has put in His Word exactly what He desires from us. And goodness, besides being a fruit of the Spirit, is something He expects of us. Indeed, we are instructed many times in Scripture to practice good works. It's an assignment from God.

For instance, consider Ephesians 2:8-10. This for me was a

life-changing excerpt from our job description because it shows me both my responsibility to grow in good works and God's grace in making that possible. This Scripture tells us that "we are [God's] workmanship, created in Christ Jesus for good works, which God prepared beforehand, that we should walk in them" (verse 10). God has ordained that we live a life dedicated to good works.

Now, this passage teaches us that only our salvation makes fulfilling this purpose possible. And…exactly how was that salvation accomplished? "Not as a result of works," says verse 9! No, our works have nothing to do with our salvation. Indeed, C.H. Spurgeon once remarked that we might better try to sail the Atlantic in a paper boat than try to get to heaven on good works! Good works do *not* result in salvation, but "by *grace* you have been saved through faith; and that not of yourselves, it is the gift of God" (Ephesians 2:8, emphasis added)—and that grace is what empowers us for good works. In other words, good works cannot save, but good works sooner or later accompany salvation.[12]

Another part of the assignment God gives you and me as members of "the household of faith" is found in Galatians 6:10. Here God expresses His desire for us to extend good works to all people—not only to other Christians, but also to those who are not. We read, "Let us do good to all men, and especially to those who are of the household of the faith." And, as Dr. Chuck Swindoll acknowledges, we won't always feel like doing good. Why? Because "our tendency [when hurt] will be anything but that [of doing good]. Instead of good, we will feel like doing evil. Fume. Swear. Scream. Fight. Pout. Get irritated. Burn up all kinds of emotional BTUs. Rather than parading through that shop-worn routine, stay quiet and consciously turn it *all* over to the Lord. Let us do good."[13] Doing good to everyone is a tall order, but the Lord delights in helping us fulfill it.

Another clause in our job description—and one of my favorite formulas for interpersonal relationships—is Luke 6:27-28. These verses reveal Jesus' rule for love in our difficult relationships. He says, "Love your enemies, do good to those who hate you, bless those who curse you, pray for those who mistreat you." In other words, we are to love those who cause us pain through the *personal* response of doing good, the *public* response of blessing, and the *private* response of praying.

Abraham Lincoln was able to do just that toward a mean and insulting man named Stanton. Lincoln definitely knew how to love his enemies as Jesus instructed, as we can see in the following account:

> No one treated Lincoln with more contempt than did Stanton. He called him "a low cunning clown," he nicknamed him "the original gorilla" and said that [one was a fool] to wander about Africa trying to capture a gorilla when he could have found one so easily at Springfield, Illinois. Lincoln said nothing. He made Stanton his war minister because he was the best man for the job and he treated him with every courtesy. The years wore on. The night came when the assassin's bullet murdered Lincoln in the theatre. In the little room to which the President's body was taken stood that same Stanton, and, looking down on Lincoln's silent face, he said through his tears, "There lies the greatest ruler of men the world has ever seen."[14]

Like Jesus said, there should never be a person whom we refuse to love. In any and every case, we are to love friend and enemy alike by our acts of goodness. Thank God that He helps us fulfill this assignment by filling us with His goodness so that we have His goodness to give to others!

Putting Goodness to Work

As you and I walk through the day-in, day-out routines and responsibilities of life, we have a variety of opportunities to choose goodness. And many of these challenges come with our various roles as women—single or married.

In fact, I find it sobering to notice how many times God specifies goodness and good works as the high calling for us as His women.

As women we are to learn goodness. In Titus 2:5 Paul writes to the new pastor Titus to make sure that the young women are taught by other women and encouraged by them to, among other things, "be...good" (Titus 2:5 KJV).

This, dear sister, is instruction for our daily relationships of home life. Older women are to encourage younger women to love their husbands and children (verse 4). Women of God are to exhibit spiritual goodness "while performing their tasks in the family...[and to] take care that the constant strain of domestic duties [did] not make them irritable or cruel. They must pray for the grace to remain kind [and good]."[15] This is sound advice!

As women we are to teach goodness. Once a younger woman learns goodness from older women, she is to take on the role of teacher herself and pass on to others what she's learned over the years. Titus was not to teach the women about their roles. Instead, he was to have the older women teach what is good and encourage the young women to be kind and good (Titus 2:3-5). This means that you and I can—and should...and *must!*—use all that we have learned to help other women understand what walking by the Spirit is all about.

As women we are to be devoted to goodness. In 1 Timothy 5, Paul describes which widows the church should care for monetarily: They were to be the widows who had a "reputation for good works" (verses 9,10). And what were some of those good works? Paul writes, "If she…[has] been the wife of one man…if she has brought up children, if she has shown hospitality to strangers, if she has washed the saints' feet, if she has assisted those in distress, and if she has devoted herself to every good work" (verses 9,10). It's plain to see that the measuring stick for the widows' goodness—and ours as well—began at home: They were to be faithful wives, wise mothers, good hosts, and kind benefactresses.[16] Oh, how I pray that you and I never overlook the importance of what goes on right in our own home! Our goodness is truly to be lived out among the people who live under our roof as well as those who enter our doors.

As women we are to adorn ourselves with goodness. In 1 Timothy 2:9-10 the apostle Paul addresses the place of women in the church. Here he writes that God's desire for women was that they adorn themselves "by means of good works, as befits women making a claim to godliness" (verse 10). Speaking of Christian women, one scholar writes that good works "create that spiritual adornment which is the real glory of the Christian woman."[17]

Good works as an adornment for a woman suggests a life of selfless devotion to others, an adornment that lies not in what she puts on, but in the loving service she gives out.[18] Clearly, God wants our good works to be our chief ornaments. They are what He wants others to notice—not our clothes and not our jewelry. These good works, these selfless deeds and sacrificial actions, will reflect our walk with God.

Enjoying a Sampling of Goodness

As you and I turn through the pages of our Bible, we find many instances of goodness.

- As we've already seen, *Dorcas* was a woman "full of good works" for the widows (Acts 9:36 KJV). In her kindness, she noticed their need, and then her goodness followed through with action and made clothes for them (verse 39).

- *The Shunammite woman,* in her kindness, noticed Elisha passing through her town. Then her goodness went into action and followed through: In addition to providing his meals, she had a small room built on top of her home so Elisha could stay there every time he came her way (2 Kings 4:8-10).

- When *Rebekah,* Isaac's future wife, arrived at the town well to draw water, she saw there a tired, old man who had just completed a 500-mile journey. In her kindness she realized how weary he was from his long trek and noticed his needs. But her goodness took him water—and also watered his ten camels. Rebekah followed through on her observations with action. She did everything she could think of to ease the old servant's life and meet his needs (Genesis 24:15-20).

- *Lydia,* on the same day she became a Christian after hearing the apostle Paul speak, realized in her kindness that Paul and his companions had no place to stay. So she acted in her newborn goodness and insisted, "Come into my house and stay" (Acts 16:15). Lydia provided for them and met their needs. She did everything she could for them.

- *Martha,* unfortunately, offers us a negative example. Oh, she did all the *deeds* of goodness, but she did them without patience or kindness or goodness. Martha crossed over the line into the works of the flesh. In our chapter on peace, we saw her complaining and out of control; "Martha the Mouth" was accusing, blaming, and slandering (Luke 10:38-42). She lived out the desires of the flesh instead of walking by the Spirit (Galatians 5:16). Martha serves as a caution signal for us, showing us how easy it is to slip from doing a good thing.

Learning from Jesus' Goodness

Of course our Jesus supplies us with the ultimate example of every grace fruit, and God's Word shows patience, kindness, and goodness all wrapped up together in Jesus. For instance, in Luke 9:51-56, our Lord is moving determinedly toward the cross. He had resolutely set His face to go to Jerusalem, where He knew He would die for mankind's sins. Jesus had sent several of His disciples ahead to make arrangements for their stay in a Samaritan village—and they did not receive Him. The Samaritans—for whom Jesus was going to die—said, in essence, "Go away. We don't want You!"

Here, my friend, is a people problem! Jesus—God's love in human flesh—moved toward Jerusalem to demonstrate, in blood, His love for sinful people. And these Samaritans refused to even welcome Him into their town for one night! But look at His disciples' reaction: "Lord, do You want us to command fire to come down from heaven and consume them?" (Luke 9:54). And now look at the Lord's response. What did He think about the disciples' suggestion? He turned and He rebuked them, saying, "You do not know what kind of spirit you are of; for the Son of Man did not come to destroy men's lives, but to save them" (verses 55-56). Then Jesus led them on to another village.

Our Jesus was patience in action. *He* was the one who had been rebuffed, not the disciples! And He was definitely a man who could avenge Himself. But He chose not to. He was also kindness personified. He wanted the best for those Samaritans. And He was Goodness-in-flesh as He kept moving to Jerusalem to die for the very people—the Samaritans and those of us like them—who had rejected Him. The disciples, however, possessed no patience. They wanted revenge, retaliation, the chance to strike back! And they possessed no kindness. They wanted the Samaritans to be punished. And they possessed no goodness. They wanted to destroy the Samaritans by calling down fire and wiping them out.

Oh, how many times we take the same approach these confused, proud, foolish disciples took and respond with antagonism! It's just so easy, isn't it? So natural…and it feels so good, so smug, so righteous! But, dear friend, when you or I are hurt, rejected, abused, or snubbed, we need to make the patience that Jesus exhibited our first action—and do nothing. This choice then gives us time (even a split second!) to pray and reflect on God's way of responding to those who cause us pain. This choice to do nothing also gives us time to plan deeds of kindness so that we can then follow through with the actions of goodness. Truly, every assault upon us gives us an opportunity to live out godliness.

Walking in Goodness

Oswald Chambers writes so beautifully, "Christian character is not expressed by good doing, but by God-likeness. It is not sufficient to do good, to do the right thing. We must have our goodness stamped by the image and superscription of God. It is supernatural all through."[19] These words offer us a healthy reminder that our goal is to grow in godliness, not just to crank out works. So I urge you to pray for God's stamp on your life as you attempt to cultivate goodness in the following ways:

- Confess any thoughts or deeds that are not kind or good. Augustine wrote, "The confession of evil works is the first beginning of good works."[20]

- Take the initiative in meeting the specific needs of others. After all, love means action.

- Forget your own comfort: "When God is at work in the believer, he desires to be good and to do good.... It becomes clear that the good life is not comfort, but godliness."[21]

- Advance the happiness of others: "Kindness is a sincere desire for the happiness of others; goodness is the activity calculated to advance their happiness."[22]

Things to Do Today to Walk in Goodness

As we near the end of our section on cultivating the actions of grace, again I want you to consider that person who challenges you the most, who causes you the most pain. And now I urge you to pour forth His goodness on the one who hurts you so deeply. Give every goodness you can think of and help him or her. Put kind thoughts into action and *do everything* God brings to your mind to do for that person. Act on His grace and then you will show forth His glory as you walk with Him.

9

Looking at Jesus' Actions

❧

Jesus, our wonderful Master and Teacher, perfectly lived out the gracious actions of godliness we've been looking at. We saw one example at the end of chapter 5 when we witnessed Jesus praying in the Garden of Gethsemane. Do you remember? It was time for Him to die for mankind's sin. In His humanness, Jesus needed to go before His all-wise Father and come to terms with this awful assignment. And so, resisting all human and fleshly urges to rebel, panic, turn, or fall apart, Jesus instead fell upon His Father's breast in prayer. Then, after a time of earnest and intense prayer, Jesus came to terms with the upcoming events, "hushed His Spirit,"[1] and rose up from the ground filled with God's love, joy, and peace. Fortified after His time of prayer and having "thoroughly equipped Himself,"[2] Jesus gathered His sleeping disciples and boldly walked through the garden gate...

...to face people. Jesus knew that people were waiting on the other side of the gate. My friend, interpersonal problems will always be a part of the challenge of living out the Christian life, but we can learn so very much from our Lord who, even at this point, magnificently displayed God's gracious response to people. Exactly who was waiting for Jesus outside the garden?

The Traitor

As He resolutely strode toward the garden entrance, Jesus said, "Behold, the one who betrays Me is at hand!" (Matthew 26:46). The Savior most definitely knew *what* was about to happen—and He also knew *who* was instrumental in the process: It was Judas. How Christ's heart must have ached as He looked into the face and eyes of Judas—one of the Twelve chosen to be the focus of His ministry of teaching, leadership, provision, and miracles; one who had been prayed for by the Savior and fed by His miraculous multiplication of loaves and fishes; one whose dirty feet had been washed by the Savior's holy hands; one who had heard the words of life and truths of God from the mouth of God Himself. Few people have tasted the privileges Judas had enjoyed on a daily basis in the presence of our loving Jesus!

Yet there Judas stood, filled with the darkness of hell itself and the evil of Satan, a traitor and a betrayer. What grief and disappointment must have filled our Lord! What heartache and sorrow must have sickened Him! A friend, a disciple, an intimate companion—now a traitor!

The Mob

And Judas was not alone. He was "accompanied by a great multitude with swords and clubs, from the chief priests and elders of the people" (Matthew 26:47). Included in this group of as many as a thousand[3] were the officers of the temple (Luke 22:52), a company of Roman soldiers, the chief priests and elders.[4]

Yes, Jesus had to deal with people. For the next 18 hours, He would face a host of hostile people—people who would abuse Him physically and verbally, people who would hurl not only insults at Him but also fists, whips, staves, hammers, and spears. Still to come were the high priest Caiaphas, the scribes, the elders, and the Council of the Sanhedrin (Matthew 26:57-60).

And there would be still more! The list of Jesus' enemies continues:

- Pilate—who would call for Jesus' death (Matthew 27:2).

- The soldiers—who would strip Him, mock Him, spit on Him, and beat Him (verses 28-30).

- The two thieves crucified with Him—one of whom would insult Him (Luke 23:39-41).

- The crowd—which would hurl abuses and wag their heads in mockery (Matthew 27:39-40).

- The disciples—who would flee, leaving Jesus even more alone (Matthew 26:56).

Truly, the forces of evil had gathered for the purpose of arresting Jesus and putting Him to death.

The Fleshly Response

As soon as Judas kissed Jesus, His enemies came and laid hands on Jesus and seized Him (Matthew 26:50). In the seconds that followed, we see (again!) the fleshly response of Jesus' disciples in sharp contrast to His gracious response of patience, kindness, and goodness.

Think for a minute about this troubling scene of Jesus' arrest. It happened under the dark cover of night. Possibly a thousand people were involved. There was confusion and panic. Emotions ran high as the Savior of the world met its evil head on.

And, in the heat of those emotions, "one of those who were with Jesus reached and drew out his sword, and struck the slave of the high priest, and cut off his ear" (verse 51). We learn from the

apostle John that this "one" is Peter (John 18:10). Peter showed
no patience. Instead, he went into action. He grabbed a sword
and swung—but, as someone notes, "What a ridiculous blow!
How like a man half-awake! Instead of the head, he only smote
the ear."[5] No gracious patience was exhibited in Peter's desire to
slash 'em, dash 'em, thrash 'em, and kill 'em! He also showed no
kindness—the kindness of God that desires the best for others.
Instead, Peter's action caused someone to suffer. And he certainly
showed no goodness—that fruit of the Spirit that also does everything for the good of others. Instead, Peter hurt someone in his
efforts to protect his Master. Peter most definitely responded in
the fleshly way. He chose the easy response. He reacted. He evi-
denced "the deeds of the flesh" (Galatians 5:19).

The Godly Response

Jesus also went into action. Notice how His response exhibited the fruit of the Spirit.

The Godly Response of Patience—First, Jesus lived out God's
perfect patience. Do you remember the definition of patience
from chapter 6? Patience is endurance when injured by others,
it is interested in their good, it is without vengeance, and it *does
nothing*. Jesus lived every aspect of this gracious fruit. Wanting
nothing done in retaliation or reaction, He told Peter, "Put your
sword back into its place" (Matthew 26:52). Although Jesus definitely could have avenged Himself, He rebuked Peter's puny
action by asking, "Do you think that I cannot appeal to My
Father, and He will at once put at My disposal more than twelve
legions of angels?" (verse 53). Instead of calling on 72,000 angels,
Jesus acted in perfect patience. He did nothing and consequently
was led away (verse 57) as a lamb to the slaughter (Isaiah 53:7).

The Godly Response of Kindness—And why did Jesus let Himself be led away? Because of His kindness. God's kindness is

concerned for the welfare of others (even one's enemies), it desires to better their lives, and it consciously *plans to do something* for them. In kindness, Jesus had "resolutely set His face to go to Jerusalem" (Luke 9:51) in the first place. In kindness, He had agonized in prayer those three long hours. And now, acting in kindness, He met the mob head on instead of fleeing. In His divine kindness, Jesus planned to do something for His enemies: He planned to die for them!

The Godly Response of Goodness—Finally, in goodness, our Savior moved into action. Goodness is active kindness and flows out of a heart that stands ready to do good. And goodness *does everything* possible to help others live well. So what did Jesus do? He turned to the man whose ear Peter had cut off, "touched his ear and healed him" (Luke 22:51). This man was one of the enemy mob. He had come to apprehend Jesus, yet now he found himself on the receiving end of Jesus' goodness. He experienced a miracle of goodness. In fact, his healing was the last service Jesus rendered before being bound. Appropriately for our Savior and Lord, "the last action of that hand, while it was still free, was one of love, one of rendering service to men."[6]

Our Response

Truly Jesus is the God of all grace who is "able to make all grace abound to you, that always having all sufficiency in everything, you [too] may have an abundance for every good deed" (2 Corinthians 9:8)! Having seen our Savior's great graciousness in horrific circumstances, how can you or I ever again lash out at others? How could we ever again be impatient with others after witnessing the beauty and grace of our Lord's patience with His killers? How could we ever again wish evil or ill upon others after watching our Savior's kindness as He walked the lonely road to Jerusalem to die for us all? And how could we ever again strike out physically or verbally at another after seeing our Savior's healing touch for an enemy? To be like Jesus requires us to be filled with God's grace—His Spirit's gifts of patience, kindness, and goodness. To respond in His way requires looking to Him to "find grace to help in time of need" (Hebrews 4:16). Let's look to Him now in prayer...

> It is in prayer, dear Father,
> That we thank You for the people in our life
> > who cause us to need Your grace so.
> We acknowledge that
> > Your patience,
> > Your kindness, and
> > Your goodness enable us to do nothing
> > harmful, to truly care, and to act out Your
> > love toward others.
> In our pain...our tears...our suffering...
> > we look to You, O heart of love.
> May we refuse to act or react until we have
> > again looked at our Savior's actions and seen
> > His patience...His kindness...His goodness.
> May we grow in these graces.
> In Jesus' name, who came not to be ministered
> > to but to minister to others...
> > even to the point of giving His life as a ransom.
> > Amen.

APPLICATIONS
of the
Fruit of the Spirit

10

Following Through in Faithfulness

❧

The fruit of the Spirit is...faithfulness.
GALATIANS 5:22

At work my husband Jim has a terrific secretary who keeps his desk in order, but at home I'm the one who ends up with that task. One evening, while I was filing some of Jim's materials, a newspaper cartoon fell out of the manila folder. Wearing a colonial general's hat made out of paper, holding a tiny wooden sword, and standing in a George Washington pose on top of a rock, Pogo was uttering the infamous words, "We have met the enemy— and they is us!"

"We have met the enemy—and they is us" is exactly how I feel many nights at the end of another day that began with such good intentions. The discouragement comes when I realize that I, too, have watched the national average of 6.4 hours of TV; that I've eaten the foods that move one to the "20 pounds overweight" category; that I have hardly touched the to-do list (I can't even find it!); or that I have failed to open my Bible. I am truly my own worst enemy when it comes to being a disciplined woman. How greatly I need the Spirit's fruit of self-control!

In this book, you and I have been on a journey to discover the meaning of each fruit of the Spirit listed in Galatians 5:22-23. First, as we learned about love and joy and peace, we grew to understand that these lovely qualities bloom with great sacrifice.

Next we dealt with the challenge of handling people the way God desires—and the way Jesus did—by looking to the Holy Spirit for His patience, kindness, and goodness.

And now we must move on to conquer the discipline of self. If you're cringing at the thought of self-discipline, know that there is hope for meeting this challenge. That hope lies in the final three aspects of the fruit of the Spirit that God has made available to us as we walk with Him—faithfulness, gentleness, and self-control (Galatians 5:22-23). These graces enable us to triumph over weakness, impulsiveness, and laziness and win over procrastination, stubbornness, and unhealthy desires. So hang on! It may be a rough road to walk, but a pattern for victory through God's Spirit awaits us at the other end. Let's begin with faithfulness.

Insights into Faithfulness

As Christians it is vitally important that God's faithfulness be a part of our character. Why? Because faithfulness marks God's presence in our life. When you and I are faithful, we show that we are born of God and belong to Him. As we walk in faithfulness, we show forth our faithful Savior to others. Faithfulness is also critical because, as someone has said, "The final criterion God will use to judge us will not be success but faithfulness."[1] Jesus also showed the seriousness of being faithful in His parable of the talents (Matthew 25:14-30). Using this story to teach the value of faithful obedience, Jesus praised those who are reliable and called them "good and faithful" (verses 21,23). Every woman who walks with God longs to hear these words said of her, especially by our Lord!

The following insights can help us in our understanding of faithfulness and our desire to walk in greater faithfulness.

Insight #1—The God of Faithfulness. From the opening page of the Bible to the last, we can see that God is faithful. As I was reading the Psalms just this morning, I was again moved by these words: "To all generations I will make known Thy faithfulness with my mouth" (89:1). Moses did just that when he praised God, exulting, "The Rock!...a God of faithfulness... is He" (Deuteronomy 32:4). As one scholar exhorts, "God is a Rock...and there should be something of the rock in us."[2] This truth about God's faithfulness, dear friend, should bring comfort to both of us. When we pause to ponder God's faithfulness, strength is infused to our sore souls and we find courage to stand on Him, the Rock. Just as Jeremiah and his people did, you and I can endure our trials by counting on God's faithfulness (Lamentations 3:22-23).

The New Testament shows us that Jesus is faithful, too. Indeed His name is "Faithful and True" (Revelation 19:11). And how did Jesus exhibit His faithfulness? His ultimate demonstration is this: "Because Jesus was faithful, He 'emptied Himself, taking the form of a bond-servant, and being made in the likeness of men. And being found in appearance as a man, He humbled Himself by becoming obedient to the point of death, even death on a cross' (Philippians 2:7-8)."[3]

I certainly know that these sacred words cause me to wonder: Am I faithfully fulfilling God's purpose for my life, just as my Lord did? Am I faithfully serving those in my path—my husband, my children, my church, my co-workers? Am I walking in humility before God so that He may exalt me (1 Peter 5:6)? Am I willing to follow in Jesus' steps of faithfulness and obedience and make every sacrifice that faithfulness requires—even that of death? When I consider these questions, I can only trust that God knows the desires of my poor, weak heart!

So, we've seen that God is faithful and Jesus is faithful. And we also know that God's Word is faithful. The aged apostle John was instructed to write down his visions because "these words are faithful and true" (Revelation 21:5). We are indeed a blessed people to be eternally experiencing the faithfulness of the Godhead and the faithfulness of the Bible!

Insight #2—The Core of Faithfulness. Faithfulness is defined as loyalty, trustworthiness, or steadfastness.[4] It is characteristic of the person who is reliable,[5] and it applies to the Christian's behavior in respect to people as well as toward God.[6] Our faithfulness to God and His will, to God and His Word, does not exclude—but includes—loyalty to others.[7] The *Ryrie Study Bible* adds that faithfulness means faithful not only in deed, but also in word.[8]

Whew! That's a lot to take in, isn't it? But this fruit of faithfulness becomes vital to us when we see that God calls us as women to be "faithful in all things" (1 Timothy 3:11). You see, faithfulness is a major distinction of Christian women and a quality God uses to benefit the church, the body of Christ. I know we've both had experiences with people who have failed to come through. We know firsthand how it feels to be disappointed or left with the full burden when we counted on someone who let us down. And…we ourselves have probably been unfaithful at times. Oh, to be more like Jesus—faithful and true!

Insight #3—The Marks of Faithfulness. What does faithfulness do? What does faithfulness in action look like? Well, if you were watching a woman who is walking with God by His Spirit, you would note these marks:

• She follows through—on whatever she has to do.

- She comes through—no matter what.

- She delivers the goods—whether a message or a meal.

- She shows up—even early so others won't worry.

- She keeps her word—her *yes* means *yes* and her *no* means *no* (James 5:12).

- She keeps her commitments and appointments—you won't find her canceling.

- She successfully transacts business—carrying out any instructions given to her.

- She discharges her official duties in the church—and doesn't neglect worship.

- She is devoted to duty—just as Jesus was when He came to do His Father's will (John 4:34).

So, my friend…take a quick inventory of your own Christian walk. Let these points stretch your understanding of the fruit of faithfulness, a fruit that is so needed in our world today! And then ask God for His strength to go to work cultivating His faithfulness in your life.

Insight #4—The Opposites of Faithfulness. A greater understanding of faithfulness comes as we consider its opposites. (You may have already thought of a few yourself!) One of those opposites is *fickle*. We've all met people who change—change their minds, change their loyalties, change their standards. Something in their nature is unstable, capricious, impulsive. Nothing seems to matter. Nothing seems too important. Nothing seems to merit commitment.

Another opposite of "faithful" is *unreliable*. An unreliable person doesn't come through, can't be depended upon, and can't be trusted with responsibility. As the saying goes, you may depend on the Lord—but may He depend on you?

Insight #5—The Essence of Faithfulness. As I considered the faithfulness of God—the strengths at the core of faithfulness, the marks of a faithful saint, and the opposites of faithfulness— I chose as my own definition the slogan "*Do it!*" or, to quote the Nike shoe ads, "*Just do it!*" Faithfulness means doing it…no matter what, doing it…regardless of feelings, moods, or desires—if the Lord wills (James 4:15).

"*Do it!*" has become my battle cry as I struggle daily with my own areas of weakness. Tiredness heads the list…followed closely by laziness. But when I make a decision to *do it* and look to God for His strength and purpose in *doing it,* He gives me the grace to have victory over both. Later we'll look more at the enemies of faithfulness, but for now let the motto "*Do it!*" move you toward greater faithfulness. Try it…for an hour, a day, a week. I think you'll amaze yourself (and others!) as they see this sturdy fruit grow in your life through the work of God's faithful Spirit.

The Need for Faithfulness

Understanding faithfulness is a good first step, but we must also realize that we have a need for it. I confess that, at the sound of the alarm clock each morning, I feel overwhelmed by the many hats I have to wear, the multitude of people I need to serve, and the variety of roles God asks me to fulfill. As women, you and I have many—*many!*—assignments from God which we cannot accomplish without faithfulness. For instance, the primary assignment for married women is the role of wife. We are to love our husband (Titus 2:4) and help him (Genesis 2:18), giving all that these two instructions entail—for life! And, if we have children, we are to love them (Titus 2:4) and bring them up in the things of the Lord (Ephesians 6:4), faithfully teaching and training them according to God's Word.

And then, whether we're married or single, the duties and responsibilities of the home demand a high level of faithfulness. The daily basics of housework most certainly require faithful diligence! In fact, one reason I feel a need to study "the most excellent woman" of Proverbs 31 (verses 10-31) is to examine up-close a woman who faithfully carries out her assignment to be a wise manager of the home. She inspires me in my *own* homemaking as she shows me the range of her skills and her attitude as she approaches her work.

As part of our home management, we also have the obligation of money management. Again, Proverbs 31 displays this wonderful woman's shrewdness and her understanding of finances. She was definitely an asset to her household as she oversaw the budget for the home and the servants. She made money, managed money, saved money, invested money, stretched money, and gave money to the poor and needy. This woman was truly a *faithful* and trustworthy steward.

As part of my home management, I also have the obligation of desk management. My desk really forces me to follow my maxim *"Do it."* I call it "the discipline of the desk" and mentally chain myself there many hours each day. Although your desk or personal work area may not require the hours that mine does as a writer, the desk is still the place where bills are paid and letters are written; the scene of much list-making, planning, and scheduling; and the setting for projects that bring us and others so much pleasure. I laughed out loud when I read this anecdote from the life of Winston Churchill: "A professional author said to [him] that he couldn't write unless the 'mood' came on him. The great statesman replied: 'No! shut yourself in your study from nine to one and make yourself write. Prod yourself!—kick yourself!—it's the only way.'"[9] That's another way of saying, "Do it!" when it comes to the desk.

And then there is our devotional life. I know that both you and I desire the mark of God's freshness on our life, and that is achieved only by faithfully going to His Word on a day-by-day basis. Just as a flower needs water to flourish, so we need to drink daily from God's living Word.

Plus God expects His children to be faithful in the church. After all, the church is where we are to minister our spiritual gifts for the good of the body of Christ (1 Corinthians 12:7). Serving God calls for faithfulness—to Him and to His call to use His gifts and serve His people.

The father of modern missions, William Carey was faithful in his service to God in India for 41 years. Do you want to know his secret? When asked the reason for his success as a missionary, he replied, "I can plod; I can persevere in any definite pursuit. To this I owe everything."[10] Imagine the effect you and I could have upon our world today if we would just faithfully plod on!

The Struggle to Be Faithful

After thinking about the need for faithfulness, I made a list of my own personal struggles to be faithful. As I look at that list, I see clearly that these struggles are against my flesh ("For the flesh sets its desire against the Spirit, and the Spirit against the flesh; for these are in opposition to one another, so that you may not do the things that you please"—Galatians 5:17). The good news is that, as we yield our flesh to God and are led by His Spirit (Galatians 5:18), we can walk in faithfulness.

But walking in God's faithfulness is a three-step operation. First, you and I must *desire* to live a godly life that manifests the graces of the Holy Spirit. Next, we need to *look* to God: His power from on high is available to us, and He gives it to us freely. Finally, we must *follow* God's Word by moving out intentionally and confidently, empowered and guided by God. This three-step process can always help us in our struggles to be faithful. Read on...

Tiredness heads my personal list of struggles, and I know from talking with the many women who cross my path that they, too, face this struggle. Tiredness says, "I can't do it." Tiredness moans, "I can't get up....I can't get up and check on the baby....I can't make it to church....I can't run the errands....I can't study....I'm just too tired!" In the flesh, we think and feel that we can't do it.

But, while tiredness says, "I can't do it," God's Word says, "I can do all things through Him who strengthens me" (Philippians 4:13). You see, my flesh and God's Word are in direct opposition! Therefore I need to follow the threestep plan. If I *desire* to be faithful, *look* to God for His promised strength (Philippians 4:13), rise up and *follow* His leading, and do it anyway, then tiredness takes flight and faithfulness takes over. It's *my* heart, but *God's* strength transforms it. It's *God's* strength, but *my* will submitting to Him. It's *God's* will filling and influencing *my* will, resulting in *God's* fruit appearing in *my* life.

Laziness is another fleshly barrier to faithfulness. While tiredness is a physical struggle, laziness is a mental one. Laziness says, "I don't want to do it." Laziness whines, "I don't want to clean the house....I don't want to cook....I don't want to get involved in a ministry....I don't want to discipline my children....I don't want to go to my Bible study....I just don't want to do it."

But, while laziness says, "I don't want to do it," God's Word beckons, "Set your mind on the things above, not on the things that are on earth" (Colossians 3:2). God shows us a better way and prompts us to change our focus: "Look not at the things which are seen, but at the things which are not seen; for the things which are seen are temporal, but the things which are not seen are eternal" (2 Corinthians 4:18). In other words, we need to get our eyes off ourselves and off the people or the event prompting the "I don't want to..." and instead look straight into the face of Jesus. I am definitely more motivated to *do it*—whatever *it* is—when I remember Jesus' words, "to the extent that you did it to one of these...*you did it to Me*" (Matthew 25:40, emphasis added).

We can learn a very valuable lesson from Edith Schaeffer, the faithful wife of theologian Francis Schaeffer. Hear her thoughts about a life of serving others from a chapter entitled "The Lost Art of Serving..." reflecting the essence of Matthew 25:40 on serving unto Jesus.

> How do I regard my having run upstairs with tea, or having served breakfast in bed, or having continued for years to do this kind of thing for a diversity of people, as well as for husband and children? How do I look at it? Do I feel like a martyr? Let me tell you exactly how I see it.
>
> First, I say silently to the Lord...: "Thank You that there is a *practical* way to serve *You* tea [or breakfast in bed, or whatever it is I am doing for someone]. There would be *no* other way of bringing You food, or doing some special thing for You. Thank You for making it so clear that as we do things that are truly in the realm of giving of ourselves in service to others, we are really doing it for You."[11]

It's sobering to realize that all you and I do is not done only for people, but for our Savior. Serving people is a primary way for us to serve our Lord. Our ultimate motivation, as Colossians 3:23 reminds us, is "Whatever you do, do your work heartily, *as for the Lord* rather than for men" (emphasis added).

Hopelessness looms large on my list of fleshly barriers to faithfulness. Hopelessness says, "It doesn't matter if I do it." As a young mother of two preschoolers, I struggled with this feeling. The need to discipline and train my children was so constant, so draining, so demanding, and progress appeared agonizingly slow. I was tempted to come to the erroneous conclusion that "It doesn't *matter* if I do it." I can also feel that way about my efforts to follow God's plan for me as a wife. Sometimes when I try so hard, an argument, tension, or misunderstanding happens anyway, and "it just doesn't seem to matter if I do it." In both instances, I'm tempted to give up and ask, "Why try?" Fear sets in—fear that I'm failing with my children and they're not going to turn out as I desire; fear that I'm failing in my marriage and it's not glorifying God as it should. But (note the three steps) my *desire* to *follow* God's plan moves me to *look* to my Lord, and He is always faithful to encourage me. "Have not I commanded you?" He reminds me. "Be strong and of good courage; be not afraid; neither be thou dismayed" (Joshua 1:9 KJV). Yes, God is faithful—and His faithfulness is expressed to me through these words which are available to me not only every morning (Lamentations 3:23) but all day long as well!

Procrastination utterly kills faithfulness with its attitude, "I'll do it later." Procrastination announces, "I'll prepare for that class later....I'll finish (or start) that chapter later....I'll reconcile the bank statement later....I'll call the plumber later....I'll do it later." And exactly what do I think will happen later? Do I really think the frenzy of life will slow down, that some magical minutes will miraculously open up, that new energy will mysteriously arrive and I'll feel like doing the task I'm putting off?

Both my husband Jim and I procrastinate more than we'd like! One day a Christian book catalog came in the mail, and I sat down to look through it (a good excuse for putting off some more worthy task). Listed in the books for sale was one entitled something like *Thirty Days to Overcoming Procrastination*, and the ad copy boasted helpful exercises that could be done for one month. I was thrilled! Here was help! But, rather than *do it now,* I procrastinated and grabbed a 3" x 5" card and jotted down the title and publisher so Jim could order the book from our church bookstore. Well, Jim then successfully procrastinated so long that, half a year later when he got around to ordering the book, it had been discontinued—thanks to the thousands of fellow procrastinators who had also put off ordering it! Oh, how we need our Lord's faithfulness. But, if we follow the three steps of faithfulness, we can win over the attitude of "I'll do it later" and walk in His faithfulness. So pray for a greater *desire* for this firm, solid fruit. Raise your eyes and *look* to God for His help. Then *follow* His Word which wisely prompts us, "Whatever your hand finds to do, verily, do it with all your might" (Ecclesiastes 9:10 KJV). *Do it* …just do it…and do it now!

Rationalization is an evil but subtle perspective on life, ministry, and responsibility that says, "Someone else will do it." Rationalization calculates, "Someone else will set up for the meeting.… Someone else will make the announcement.…Someone else will lead the discussion.…Someone else will do it." The godly woman who is faithful is "faithful in *all* things" (1 Timothy 3:11, emphasis added), all of the time no matter what. She is faithful as a servant in the church, as a member of a group, as a person with a leadership assignment. She is faithful as a wife and a mother, responding positively, enthusiastically, and energetically to those job assignments from God. She is faithful as a roommate, willingly doing her part of the work. She is faithful on the job, making sure she fulfills her assignments there.

A faithful woman will successfully defeat the unfruitful thought processes that lead to rationalizing, "Someone else will do it." How? By *desiring* to grow in faithfulness, by *looking* to God's Spirit to supply His faithfulness in weakness, and by *following* God's call that we be faithful in Christ Jesus (Ephesians 1:1) and faithful until death (Revelation 2:10). The way I chip away at rationalization is very simple: I try to be faithful for one day only. My goal each day is to be able to put my head on my pillow at night and thank God for helping me to be faithful to the tasks He gave me—today! Try this exercise yourself. Just for today, whatever responsibility you have, *do it*. This is a basic but very practical method for growing in godliness.

Apathy also gets in the way of our faithfulness. Apathy says, "I don't care if I do it." Apathy shrugs, "I don't care if the dishes get done....I don't care if I'm a good mom or wife....I don't care if I read my Bible....I don't care if I grow....I don't care if I'm faithful....I don't care if I do it." Apathy is a spiritual numbness that creeps in and corrupts the good that God intends for our life and the good that He wants us to accomplish for Him and His kingdom. But once again there is hope for this deadly perspective as you and I force our gaze off ourselves and *look* instead to our Father and His purpose for our life, as we turn our *desire* heavenward instead of inward, and as we *follow* in Jesus' steps, our Savior who lived "not...to be served, but to serve, and to give His life a ransom for many" (Mark 10:45)—including you and me.

If you, dear friend, are suffering from the crippling effects of apathy, won't you please stir up your heart? Do whatever it takes! Begin by remembering that Jesus' faithfulness accomplished your salvation. His faithfulness to die on the cross achieved eternal life for you. Ask Him to help you be more like Him and to help you cultivate His faithfulness.

Rebellion is the attitude that frightens me most. Rebellion says, "I won't do it." Rebellion stubbornly states, "I won't do what the Bible says....I won't do the laundry....I won't do what my husband asks....I won't do what the counselor advised....I won't do it." Rebellion is a hardness that we should fear because, as the Bible teaches, "The man [or woman] who hardens his [or her] neck…will suddenly be broken beyond remedy" (Proverbs 29:1). There is no deadlier attitude of the heart than rebellion— whether blatant, open, outspoken rebellion or quiet rebellion which simply and silently goes about life in its own way.

Pause now and take your pulse. Is there any part of God's Word that you know you need to heed? Is there any secret compartment in your soul that is not obeying God's ways? Is there any godly counsel you've been given that you're failing to follow? I plead with you to *look* to the Lord, ask Him to give you the *desire* to be faithful to His Word, and then *follow* in His path of obedience. Pray along with David, "Search me, O God, and know my heart; try me, and know my thoughts; and see if there be any wicked way in me" (Psalm 139:23-24 KJV).

Are you wondering where you can get the strength necessary for all this faithfulness? Where you can get the desire? Where you can get much-needed help? Our great God has made all we need to be faithful available to us through His grace. He wants us to do what David, the shepherd-king of Israel, did when he "strengthened himself in the Lord his God" (1 Samuel 30:6). David repeatedly declared, "The Lord is the strength of my life" (Psalm 27:1 KJV).

Praise God that you and I can go to Him when we are too tired, too lazy, too uncommitted, too sick, or feeling too sorry for ourselves. In fact, moments like these are precisely when we need to call upon God and be filled with His faithfulness. We can go to Him and ask Him to fill us with His strength. We can find in Him the strength (*His* strength), the vision (*His* vision), and thereby the faithfulness (*His* faithfulness). Indeed, He is waiting to give us His faithfulness.

Women Who Were Faithful to Jesus

A great source of encouragement to be faithful is found in the extraordinary faithfulness of the women at the tomb. These dear women had faithfully ministered to the needs of the Savior by serving Him and financially supporting His ministry (Luke 8:3). But their most heroic act of faithfulness began as they followed Jesus on His last journey from Galilee to Jerusalem—on His journey to the cross, a journey that finally found this loyal band of ladies with Jesus the entire day of His crucifixion and death.

I've always admired these women. I mean, just think about what that last day in Jesus' life was like, that horrendous day the women spent at the foot of the cross! The darkness (Luke 23:44), the agony of Jesus' suffering, the mocking and jeering of the crowd, the brutality of their Lord being beaten, crowned with thorns, nailed to a cross, and pierced in His side with a spear (John 19:34), an earthquake (Matthew 27:51)—it just seems to be more than a person could bear!

Well, we know the disciples couldn't handle it! They had already denied their Savior and fled (Mark 14:50). But, in faithfulness, this sorrowing group of holy women stood as near as they could to comfort Jesus by their presence in the closing agonies of the crucifixion (Luke 23:49). If I had been one of those women, I probably would have gone home after all these gruesome events, taken three aspirin, and gone to bed.

But not these faithful women. They stayed—to the end— the bitter, awful, gruesome end! Luke reports, "The women who accompanied Him from Galilee were standing at a distance, seeing these things" (23:49). And their faithfulness did not end with Jesus' death. They waited at the cross to see what was done with His body, and then they followed and saw the tomb and how His body was laid (verse 55). Then, surely weary after a long and agonizing day, these women returned home to perform two more acts of faithfulness. First, they prepared spices and perfumes to properly anoint Jesus' body (verse 56). (And, according to Jewish Sabbath law, these preparations had to be completed before sundown!) And then these women practiced their faithfulness in another way: "On the Sabbath they rested according to the commandment" (verse 56). They were faithful to Jesus, and they were faithful to God and His holy Law.

But still we've not seen the end of their faithfulness. Hear the story from Mark:

> And when the Sabbath was over, Mary Magdalene, and Mary the mother of James, and Salome, brought spices, that they might come and anoint Him. And very early on the first day of the week, they came to the tomb when the sun had risen. And they were saying to one another, "Who will roll away the stone for us from the entrance of the tomb?" (16:1-3).

Do you see the marks of faithfulness in these women, dear reader? The list is long. Their beloved Jesus is dead, but hardly forgotten because they were faithful friends—faithful to His last breath...and beyond. They prepared the anointing elements in advance (not putting it off until later). They rose early (not sleeping in due to laziness, depression, or exhaustion). They went ahead to the tomb even though they knew a massive, immovable stone had been rolled in front of the entrance (no rationalizing or excuses). Even as they went, they wondered how they were going to gain access to Jesus' body, but they didn't let the thought of an obstacle deter them. They went to the tomb anyway. They followed through. They showed up. And they went early. On that morning after the Sabbath, these women went into action. These women "went with the Lord into the shadows,"[12] so to speak. Their friend still needed their ministry even though He was dead.

Whenever I'm exhausted, stretched to the limit, and tempted to give up or wait until tomorrow, I think of these magnificent women. Their love for God overruled their emotional and physical tendencies and enabled them to faithfully do the right thing. *Nothing* kept these ladies from fulfilling what they considered to be their faithful duty to a friend.

Walking in Faithfulness

I hope that after such powerful examples of faithfulness—and from a group of women who are just like you and me!—that you, too, feel the need to pause…and ponder. We *must* respond! We *must* wonder, how can we become more faithful? How can we walk in this grace, too? What can help us to cultivate God's faithfulness in our life?

Well, God's Word comes to our rescue with a few practical suggestions.

- Call upon God in prayer. "On the day I called Thou didst answer me: Thou didst make me bold with strength in my soul" (Psalm 138:3).

- Be faithful in small things. "He who is faithful in a very little thing is faithful also in much; and he who is unrighteous in a very little thing is unrighteous also in much" (Luke 16:10).

- Rely on God's strength. "I can do all things through Him who strengthens me" (Philippians 4:13).

- Fight self-indulgence. "I buffet my body and make it my slave" (1 Corinthians 9:27).

- Eliminate laziness and idleness. "[She] does not eat the bread of idleness" (Proverbs 31:27).

- Begin at home. "She looks well to the ways of her household" (Proverbs 31:27).

- Be faithful in all things. "Women must…be…faithful in all things" (1 Timothy 3:11).

• Become a "hero." I close this chapter with a prayer that the following definition of a "hero" will move you—as it has me—to desire greater faithfulness.

The Hero

The hero does not set out to be one. He is probably more surprised than others by such recognition. He was there when the crisis occurred...and he responded as he always had in any situation. He was simply doing what had to be done! Faithful where he was in his duty there...he was ready when the crisis arose. Being where he was supposed to be...doing what he was supposed to do...responding as was his custom...to circumstances as they developed...devoted to duty—he did the heroic![13]

11

Growing Strong Through Gentleness

❧

The fruit of the Spirit is...gentleness.

GALATIANS 5:22-23

O f all the blossoms along the path we walk with God, the flower of gentleness appears so fragile, yet as we'll soon see, it develops out of the strongest of underground root systems. Before I began teaching about the fruit of the Spirit, I meditated on gentleness for one whole year—and that was one entire year devoted to cultivating gentleness in my life. Then, as I've written this book and continued my study, God has given me a second year to think about gentleness.

Come along with me and find out what makes the flower of gentleness bloom.

The Meaning of Gentleness

As you know, in this section you and I are looking at the three graces that call us to discipline ourselves in our pursuit of godliness. As we learned in the previous chapter, God's faithfulness is cultivated in us as we "do it"—as we do whatever lies in our path that must be done. And we discovered, too, how heavily we must lean upon God's strength and how deeply we must reach down inside ourselves to make the effort to follow through, to come through, to become more reliable and trustworthy. Now, as we turn to gentleness, we quickly learn that we have to depend again on God.

Gentleness means to be gentle or meek, to be lowly or humble.[1] It is a form of self-control which Christ alone can give,[2] and it manifests itself in a submissive spirit toward both God and man.[3] Gentleness is also the opposite of self-reliant arrogance.[4] And, as you'll discover, gentleness is truly grown in a hothouse—and there's a high price to pay to cultivate its bloom!

Just why is gentleness so costly?

1. *Gentleness Means Trusting the Lord*—Just as we trust the Lord for every fruit of the Spirit, so we trust Him for this one, too. In Matthew 5:5, Jesus says, "Blessed are the gentle, for they shall inherit the earth." William Hendriksen had this to say about Jesus' words:

> "The meek" [or gentle] describes the person who is not resentful. He bears no grudge. Far from mulling over injuries received, he finds refuge in the Lord and commits his way entirely to him....He has learned to take joyfully "the plundering of his possessions, knowing that he has a better possession and an abiding one" (Hebrews 10:34). Yet *meekness is not weakness*....It is submissiveness under provocation, the willingness rather to *suffer* than to *inflict* injury. The meek [or gentle] person leaves everything in the hand of him who loves and cares.[5]

It helps to note first what gentleness isn't: It is *not* resentful, it bears *no* grudge, and it is *not* involved in mulling over injuries. And what does gentleness do instead? It finds refuge in the Lord and His ways. It endures plundering, provocation, and suffering in humble submission to an all-wise, caring Father, trusting totally in the love of God.

But, we instantly wonder, *how* can anyone bear plundering, provocation, suffering, and ill-treatment? For me, the answer boils down to one word—faith. The invisible root system of gentleness goes deep into the rich soil of faith. Faith believes that everything that happens in our life is allowed by God and that He is able to help us handle our situation. Our faith in the God behind this truth keeps us from struggling and fighting because faith believes that God will fight *for* us (Psalm 60:12).

Now do you see why I've been at work cultivating this fruit for two years? I have the feeling I'll be doing so for many more!

But how about you, precious traveller along life's way? Does your life show the fruit of gentleness? Where are you failing to submit to God and His management of your life? Do you consider God's meekness to be weakness? Do you generally bear grudges toward others, contemplate revenge, think vengeful thoughts? Or are you one who can look beyond the injury inflicted by another to the God of wisdom who uses pain in your life so that you might bear the mark of His Spirit in a mighty way? Whisper a prayer to God with me now and ask His blessing as you seek to bear any harshness in life with His Spirit of gentleness, trusting in Him.

2. Gentleness Means Submitting to the Master—Commentator William Barclay offers another picture of gentleness when he explains, "What throws most light on [the meaning of gentleness] is that the adjective...is used of an animal that has been tamed and brought under control."[6] This definition, along with the fact that gentleness is highly revered by God in His women (1 Peter 3:4), caused me to search a little further—which revealed some startling concepts.

- The word *tame*, which is the opposite of wild, describes one accustomed to control by another.

- The word *tame* suggests one whose will has been broken or who has allowed himself or herself to be dominated by the will of another.

- The tame person, therefore...

    —Has been toned down and exhibits complete dependence on another.

    —Has yielded all will to another's control.

    —Unquestioningly and humbly obeys what is ordered and accepts what is given.

    —Is docile and obedient and pliable, as opposed to fierce.

    —Is easy to work with and to be with.[7]

Perhaps (like me) you're not sure you like what you're reading or what it implies!

But it helps us to think about gentleness in terms of submitting to our Master, the Lord Jesus. Don't you desire to be controlled by Him? Don't you truly yearn for Him to take complete charge of your life, to lead and guide you, to protect and care for you as you follow Him unquestioningly in faith? Don't you want to be easy to work with and be with? As one believer observed, "What makes humility [or gentleness] so desirable is the marvelous thing it does to us: It creates in us a capacity for the closest possible intimacy with God."[8] To belong totally to the Master, to want only His will, to depend completely on Him, and to yield humbly to Him and His ways brings great intimacy with God.

So breathe a huge sigh of *release* and hand over to God any part of your life that you have not yet given to Him. Thank Him—as your Master and as the Master Gardener—that He is able to care for it. Allow yourself the joy of being mastered by the Master.

3. *Gentleness Means Following Christ's Example*—I have a true confession to make: As the definition of gentleness became clearer…and tougher, I felt more and more hopeless. But when I saw in God's Word that Jesus was gentle, the meaning of gentleness became much clearer.

Our Lord, the King of kings and Lord of lords, rode on a colt as He approached Jerusalem for the last time (Matthew 21:7). This was the fulfillment of a prophecy from Zechariah 9:9 which said, "Behold, your King is coming to you, *gentle*, and mounted on a donkey, even on a colt, the foal of a beast of burden" (Matthew 21:5, emphasis added). Jesus came not as a storming conqueror or a battling king, but as the King who is meek, gentle, peaceful, gracious.[9]

Hear how Jesus describes Himself in yet another passage from Matthew: "Take My yoke upon you," He says, "and learn from Me, for I am *gentle* and humble in heart" (11:29, emphasis added). Dear sister, we follow Jesus' example of gentleness when we, like Him, find refuge in God and commit our way to Him. Jesus' gentleness was grounded in a complete trust in His loving Father, and ours can be, too, as we cultivate gentleness by following His example.

4. *Gentleness Means Bowing the Soul*—I also found a lovely word picture that helped me with gentleness. The Old Testament term for gentleness, *anah*,[10] describes a mature, ripened shock of grain with its head bent low and bowed down. Just think for a moment on the beauty of this word picture. As wheat grows, the young sprouts rise above the rest. Their heads shoot up the highest because no grain has yet formed. In their immaturity, little

fruit, if any, has appeared. But, as time passes and maturity sets in, fruit comes forth—so much of it that the burdened stalk bends and its head sinks lower and lower—and the lower the head, the greater the amount of fruit.

Oh, how I want to be this kind of Christian—a Christian with a lowered head, seasoned and mature, well past the stages of arrogance, pride, and vain emptiness. I yearn for the beauty of prostrating my soul before my Lord and bending in need toward my God!

5. *Gentleness Means Putting on a Gentle Spirit*—Wearing this gracious garment calls for a decision from us. As I mentioned earlier, God loves the quality of gentleness in His women. Look at these "elements" from 1 Peter 3:1-6:

Verse 1 speaks of *the element of submission:* "In the same way, you wives, be submissive to your own husbands." Although this particular verse focuses on submission in marriage, the exhortation appears in a very long passage on submission of all kinds. All Christians are to submit themselves for the Lord's sake to every human institution in government (2:13), servants are to be submissive to their masters with all respect (2:18), Christ submitted without a word to His tormentors (2:21-25), and wives are encouraged to be submissive to their own husbands (3:1).

Verses 1a-2 point to *the element of behavior,* suggesting that husbands "may be won without a word by the behavior of their wives as they observe [their wives'] chaste and respectful behavior." What is the behavior of gentleness? Peter says it is God-fearing and blameless conduct. It is behavior that refuses to fight, refuses to give in to anger, refuses all thoughts of violence and vengeance, and refuses to assert itself. And, beloved, we can live this out only when we rest in God's sovereignty and are confident that He controls each and every situation in our life.

Verses 3-4 address *the element of the heart:* "And let not your adornment be merely external—braiding the hair, and wearing gold jewelry, or putting on dresses; but let it be the hidden person of the heart, with the imperishable quality of a gentle and quiet spirit, which is precious in the sight of God." Rather than being obsessed with our external appearance, Peter says you and I are to be concerned with our internal condition, the condition of our heart. The phrase "hidden person of the heart" refers to the personality of the Christian woman, which is made beautiful by the ministry of the Holy Spirit glorifying the Lord Jesus and manifesting Him in and through her life.[11]

And such a heart, Peter writes, should reflect a gentle and quiet spirit. "Gentle" (which is the same Greek word used in the list of the fruit of the Spirit) refers to docile and gentle cooperation, and "quiet" refers to the acceptance of life in general.[12] Put differently, "gentle" means not creating disturbances, and "quiet" means bearing with tranquility the disturbances caused by others.[13] I must say that since discovering these simple definitions, I've been praying for daily strength from God needed not to create disturbances and not to react to any disturbances created by others.

Verse 5 instructs us in *the element of trust:* "For in this way in former times the holy women also, who [trusted (KJV)] in God, used to adorn themselves, being submissive to their own husbands." Again, faith is the only way to walk in this way—a trust that looks to God in hope, and is directed towards Him and rests in Him.[14]

Verse 6 closes with *the element of faith:* "Thus Sarah obeyed Abraham, calling him lord, and you have become her children if you do what is right without being frightened by any fear." You and I put our faith into practice as we graciously accept the details of our life which contribute to a gentle and quiet spirit.

As women of God, we are to put on all these elements of gentleness (submission, behavior, heart, trust, and faith) just as we adorn our body with clothing every day. Just as we visit the closet each morning to select garments that are appropriate, we must visit God in the prayer closet and don the garment of a gentle and quiet spirit, which is rare and precious, truly beyond price.

6. *Gentleness Means "Take It"*—My personal definition of the woman who is practicing gentleness or meekness is that she will *take it*. And what is it she takes? She bears with tranquility the disturbances others create. She endures ill treatment. She withstands misunderstandings. Carrying the image of Jesus and His suffering in her mind and heart, she takes it, thus cultivating the fruit of God's gentleness.

I know this is hard to swallow, and there are obvious moral exceptions. And, of course, we should be asking God for His wisdom (James 1:5). But, dear reader, please open your heart and mind to the beauty of this fruit. God so desires gentleness to characterize our lives! Listen to Andrew Murray's thoughts on gentleness and what it means to take it:

> [Gentleness] is perfect quietness of heart. It is for me to have no trouble; never to be fretted or vexed or irritated or sore or disappointed. It is to expect nothing, to wonder at nothing that is done to me, to feel nothing done against me. It is to be at rest when nobody praises me and when I am blamed or despised....It is the fruit of the Lord Jesus Christ's redemptive work on Calvary's cross, manifest in those of His own who are definitely in subjection to the Holy Spirit.[15]

Another believer writes these words about the strength that comes from gentleness:

[Gentleness] is...first and chiefly towards God. It is that temper of spirit in which we accept [God's] dealings with us as good, and therefore without disputing or resisting....[It is a humble heart] which... does not fight against God and...struggle and contend with Him. This meekness, however, being first of all a meekness before God, is also such in the face of men, even evil men, out of a sense that these [evil men] with the insults and injuries which they may inflict, are permitted and employed by Him.[16]

Yes, it's true that in the eyes of the world, gentleness may look like weakness, but producing this fruit calls for the greatest of strength! Indeed, gentleness has been called "the fruit of power."[17] That's why I entitled this chapter "Growing Strong Through Gentleness."

The Posture of Gentleness

Here's another word picture to help us: One day while I was studying Proverbs 3:5—"Trust in the Lord with all your heart"— I glimpsed a fresh insight into how gentleness and meekness can be nurtured. The Hebrew word for "trust" originally expressed the idea of helplessly lying facedown.[18] But practicing this posture of trust calls for complete reliance on Jehovah. It calls for an absolute confidence that God alone knows the right way to the right ends and what benefits us. It also comes with the certainty that God is able to free us from that which does us harm. Therefore this trust—this placing of our total confidence wholly in God—is the source of gentleness or meekness. We find ourselves able to helplessly lie facedown only because we trust God's wisdom *and* His ability to protect and defend us.

Clearly, this picture of trust reveals that gentleness is opposite to much that our world exalts. Gentleness is the opposite of

self-assertiveness and self-interest. It is the opposite of violence
and outbursts of anger, the evidence of God at work in our life.

And here's something else to help us with our posture: Gentleness is not only outward toward people. Nor is it a natural disposition. And it's not what some have chosen to call "a phlegmatic
temperament." No…gentleness (like all of the fruit of the Spirit)
has to do with our relationship with God and is basically a submissiveness to the will of God. As we learned earlier, faithfulness
will do it but gentleness will *take* it. And we will take it from the
hands of others because we know God's sovereign and holy hand
rests upon our life and He will never remove it!

Consider, too, the hothouse conditions that grow God's gentleness. Gentleness is required when wrong is inflicted upon us
and when we are suffering the heat of ill treatment. And what
does gentleness do under those conditions? It lies helplessly facedown. It bends, it bows, it lowers its head before the Father. It
submits, it accepts, and it humbles itself under the mighty hand
of God: Gentleness *takes it.*

Gentleness accomplishes all of this by not fighting. And you
and I take a giant step toward cultivating gentleness in our life
when we decide that we will not fight or contend or resist what
God is doing in our life. We must give up disputing, complaining, murmuring, and grumbling. After all, why should we do
these things if God is in control and God is allowing these trying situations?

Are you familiar with Psalm 46:10? Many of us know this
verse as "Be still, and know that I am God" (KJV). But did you
know that the Hebrew for "Be still" means "Stop striving"? One
scholar translates this rebuke, "Quiet!…Leave off!"[19] In essence
God is telling us, "Stop it! Stop all your warlike activity,[20] for it is
I, God, who is doing this!" We are to "cease striving" (NASB), to
stop fighting, and instead take it—whatever it is—as being held
in the hand of our sovereign and loving God. Then, as we practice

this posture of a trusting heart before God and rely on Him for His wisdom and mercy and protection, we indeed grow strong through gentleness.

Demonstrations of Gentleness

These are deep and thought-provoking truths, aren't they, my friend? But aren't you glad God gives us examples of other women who have grappled with—and grown in— gentleness? Let's take a quick look at a few:

We've already met *Hannah*. Hannah found herself the daily prey of her husband's other wife, who provoked her year after year because she had no children (1 Samuel 1:67). Can you imagine yourself in a situation where you are purposefully vexed by another person day after day, year after year? How would you respond, how would you act, what would you do?

Well, Hannah shows us the gentle response. In her great distress, she prayed to the Lord (verse 10). Instead of getting into a verbal battle or succumbing to tattling, plotting, or scheming to get even, Hannah chose to take it and she told the Lord instead. And what enabled her to take it? Her God in whom she put her faith. She could leave her unjust mistreatment with Him— knowing that He would judge righteously (1 Peter 2:23).

Mary, the mother of our Lord Jesus, also shows us an example of gentleness. You probably know her story well—by a creative act of the Holy Spirit, Mary conceived and bore the baby Jesus. But did you know that many thought of Mary as a fornicator? Joseph, her husband-to-be, wanted to privately break their engagement (Matthew 1:19), and certain Jewish authorities referred to Jesus as one born of fornication (John 8:41). As Mary's life illustrates, exceptional privilege often goes hand in hand with sacrifice and the first thing Mary sacrificed was her reputation.[21]

Pastor and radio teacher J. Vernon McGee wrote this about Mary's submission to God's will: "She told the angel, 'Be it unto me according to thy word.' At that very moment a cloud came over her life, and that cloud was there until the Lord Jesus Christ came back from the dead. The resurrection of Christ proves His virgin birth. It was questioned until then."[22] What options were available to the young, single, and pregnant Mary? She could have tried to explain, she could have told what happened, and she could have bragged. But instead, the gentle and meek Mary took it. In fact, for 33 years she silently endured the name-calling and the misunderstanding (John 8:41).

Mary of Bethany is another woman who models gentleness for us. In a touching scene of devotion, Mary anointed Jesus' feet with costly perfume and spikenard and then wiped His feet with her hair (John 12:1-8). But then a problem arose. As the house filled with the fragrance of the perfume, Judas criticized Mary in front of everyone assembled when he sneered, "Why was this perfume not sold for three hundred denarii, and given to poor people?" (verse 5). As one commentator notes, "While the odor of the spikenard was sweet to many, it smelled of waste to others. Judas with his calculating mind quickly figured up the cost of it and called it wasted on Jesus."[23]

How would you feel, precious one, if, after pouring out your heart in worship of your Savior, you were criticized publicly? And how would you respond? Our Mary responded with godly silence. Her good intentions were misinterpreted and she was criticized—yet she took it. She quietly bowed her head and bore the pain of public ridicule...and trusted in God instead. In gentleness and meekness, Mary took it.

And what happened when she totally trusted in God, when she made the decision to respond in gentleness and take it? *God* came to her rescue! In Mary's situation, Jesus Himself shielded her against the criticism and spoke in her defense. Although Mary's good intentions were interpreted the wrong way, Jesus knew her motives…and He not only defended her, but He praised her.

Moses is another saint who teaches us much about finding strength in gentleness. As you know, God chose Moses to lead His people out of Egypt and into the Promised Land. But as Moses led, the people constantly murmured and complained against him, blaming him for all of their difficult conditions. Just look at a partial list!

- When there was no water, the people grumbled at Moses. And how did Moses respond? "He cried out to the Lord" (Exodus 15:22-25).

- After God's people failed to trust Him the first time there wasn't any water, He tried His people again in the same way. How did they handle the test this time? The people quarreled with Moses. And how did Moses respond? "Moses cried out to the Lord" (Exodus 17:1-4).

- When giants were discovered in the new land, once again all the sons of Israel grumbled against Moses and Aaron. And, once again, true to their former practices, "Moses and Aaron fell on their faces" before the Lord (Numbers 14:2-5).

- Finally, in utter rebellion, the people assembled together against Moses and Aaron. And yet again, "when Moses heard this, he fell on his face" (Numbers 16:3-4).

Did you notice Moses' pattern for handling strife? When the people complained, Moses didn't argue with them, reason with them, defend himself, or get into any kind of struggle with them. Instead, he took it. He silently endured their attack and cried unto the Lord. Moses took it—and he took it on his face, prostrate before God. Moses took it—and took it to God, appealing to God and waiting on Him to come to his rescue in these unjustified attacks.

One final attack on Moses bears looking at, and that incident—in Numbers 12—had to do with family tension (both you and I know how warm things can get in the hothouse of family relationships!). Here, Aaron (who helped Moses lead God's people) and Miriam confronted their brother Moses about his marriage to a Cushite woman (verse 1) and accused him of pride. And Moses responded with gentleness. As one Bible teacher explains, "Moses did not defend himself. Because of his humility and his gentle meekness, he did not try to justify himself or to put his brother and sister down. He knew he was being falsely criticized, and that the truth would become evident."[24]

And Moses' innocence *did* become evident: "God stepped into the scene immediately, no doubt before Moses even cried out for help. He honored Moses' response, his humility, his meekness, his willingness to bear this false accusation without a counter attack. God dealt with Aaron and Miriam....God made things right for Moses."[25] Hear God's evaluation of Moses' heart and character: "Now the man Moses was very humble [meek, KJV), more than any man who was on the face of the earth" (Numbers 12:3). Moses lived out the grace of gentleness: He took it and did nothing, trusting everything to God's able care.

I personally find the example of these saints overwhelming. I think, "I could never be like that." But at the same time I'm thankful for them. Each of these people cultivated their godly response to ridicule and suffering in the same way that we do, beloved, and, as a result, each of them grew strong through gentleness.

As I said at the beginning of this chapter, the flower of gentleness appears to be so fragile, yet it develops out of the strongest of underground root systems—out of a life hidden in God and lived in His presence, a life that lowers its head, falls on its face, and helplessly lies facedown. We can take it, dear one—we can live out gentleness—only when we stretch our roots down deep into the soil of trust and faith until we touch the heart of God and the Rock of Ages.

My prayer is that this chapter has encouraged you to bear with tranquility the ill treatment of others as you wait to see what God will do on your behalf. As the Author of every situation in your life, He is also the Finisher of those very situations. And if—and when—He chooses to step in, *He* is wholly glorified because it is evident to all that *He* came to your rescue. And if He chooses not to step in, He is equally glorified by your gentleness because only the grace and power of God Himself *in* you can enable you to take it.

Yes, but How?

So what can you and I do to walk in gentleness? How can we become more like Hannah, Mary, Mary of Bethany, and Moses?

1. Accept—Accept everything in your life as allowed by God.

2. Pray—Prayer develops the proper posture of gentleness in us—the habits of bowing, bending, kneeling, yielding, and submitting to God.

3. Refuse to complain and grumble—To complain, one wise believer notes, "is an accusation against God. It questions God's wisdom and God's good judgment. God has always equated complaining with unbelief...[because] to complain is to doubt God. It is the same thing as suggesting that God really doesn't know what He's doing."[26]

4. Refuse to manipulate—Let God resolve the issue for you. Put your faith in Scriptures like these:

Psalm 60:12—"Through God we shall do valiantly, and it is He who will tread down our adversaries."

Psalm 37:6-7—"And [God] will bring forth your righteousness as the light, and your judgment as the noonday. Rest in the Lord and wait patiently for Him; do not fret."

Psalm 57:2—"I will cry to God Most High, to God who accomplishes all things for me."

Psalm 138:8—"The Lord will accomplish what concerns me."

Taking the First Step

If you can, take a giant first step and identify the greatest issue in your life—something from the past, or some current situation that God is asking you to live with, to bear, to take. Then grab the garment of God's gentleness and meekness and put it on. Adorn yourself with this spirit of loveliness, His spirit of gentleness. And then bow your head in the posture of prayer. Allow yourself to lie facedown and trust in the Lord. Wait for His action and His solution. Truly, this fruit of gentleness is the fruit of power—and it is grown in us as we walk by the Spirit.

12

Winning the Battle of Self-Control

The fruit of the Spirit is...self-control.

GALATIANS 5:22-23

It was Friday night. Normally our church doesn't have services on Friday evenings, but our sanctuary was packed. Jim and I were sitting in the second row with our two daughters and The Master's College students who attended our Bible study. The crowd of thousands was stirring in anticipation. For me, the moment was a bit unreal. I had heard about the speaker from my first days as a Christian. I had read his classic book *Spiritual Leadership* and had studied his leadership of Overseas Missionary Fellowship. And now J. Oswald Sanders was going to speak to us in person! It was one of those once-in-a-lifetime experiences.

As Dr. Sanders mounted the five steps leading up to the pulpit, we held our breath. This saint of 92 years needed assistance. But, amazingly, as he finished his greetings and turned in his tattered Bible to begin teaching God's Word, strength and vigor came to him from the Holy Spirit, and he seemed transformed before us. We were witnessing God's power in the life of a man who had dedicated his many decades to serving and loving the Lord, a man who had walked with God for close to a century.

Dr. Sanders had spoken at the chapel service the day before, and Jim had asked him to autograph his worn copy of *Spiritual Leadership*. Jim has used this book for several decades to disciple and train men for leadership. And just as Jim had already realized, the rest of us knew this evening that we were in the presence of a man who lived out the life principles of his book.

Do you ever wonder how we can, too, grow to the spiritual stature of a saint like J. Oswald Sanders? I think the answer to that question is revealed when we consider the character quality he placed first in importance. Hear these words from his chapter entitled "Qualities Essential to Leadership":

> It has been well said that the future is with the disci-plined, and that quality has been placed first in our list, for without it the other gifts, however great, will never reach their maximum potential. Only the dis-ciplined person will rise to his highest powers. He is able to lead because he has conquered himself.[1]

Conquering one's self is what the Spirit's fruit of self-control is all about. This important gift from God is another key which, when turned, ignites the power that fuels the fruit of the Spirit. You see, self-control touches off the spiritual energy needed to kindle all of the Christian life. Let me try to show you how.

Reviewing God's Fruit

Think about the importance of self-control for a moment. I can know all about love and what it does and I can have the desire to love, but God's self-control helps me to live out that love. The same is true for joy and peace. I know I need to offer the sacrifice of praise when my heart is breaking and I want to feel self-pity, but turning the key of self-control enables God's grace to flow in me and lift that praise. Likewise, when I feel a tremendous urge to panic and fall apart, the Spirit's self-control holds me together so that I can turn to the Lord, trust Him, and experience His peace.

Patience, kindness, and goodness are also powered by the Spirit's self-control. When, for instance, every fiber of my flesh wants to be angry or get upset, the Spirit's self-control gives me God's grace to do nothing, to be patient. When hurtful circumstances make it hard for me to care about other people, only the Spirit's self-control can help me extend the godly response of kindness. And to display God's goodness—to be active in making the lives of other people easier—I once again need the Spirit's self-control.

Having just read about faithfulness and gentleness, you know how much of the Spirit's self-control it takes to follow through in faithfulness when laziness and selfishness come so easily. And we learned that gentleness takes it—but only God's self-control can give me the strength to take it.

We've come a long way together in our walk along the path of understanding the fruit of the Spirit, haven't we? Together we've learned—and, I pray, grown—as, with each new fruit, God has challenged us in deeper ways. And now the final fruit on God's list, self-control, helps it all happen. The fruit of self-control is so powerful, so essential to the Christian life, such a rock-solid foundation for our journey to be like Christ (and one that I need so badly!). "But how," we wonder, "can we ever get a grip on something this large, this important?" It helps first to get a grip on a better understanding of what self-control means.

What Is Self-Control?

In the previous chapter, the apostle Peter described the grace of gentleness as an adornment we wear when we are walking by the Spirit. However, the spiritual clothing of self-control seems

more like armor! Indeed, to practice self-control will require putting on battle gear and donning a warrior's mentality. You'll soon
see why.

To begin, the Greek root of "self-discipline" implies self-
restraint of one's desires and lusts.[2] Plato used this term to describe
the person who has mastered his desires and love of pleasure.[3]
Self-control is the controlling power of the will under the operation of the Spirit of God,[4] literally a holding in of one's self with
a firm hand by means of the Spirit.[5] In simple terms, self-control
is the ability to keep one's self in check.[6]

Did you notice the two common denominators in these
definitions? One is the control of the self—*self*-restraint, *self*-
government, and *self*-command.[7] The second common thread is
the object of control—our passions, appetites, pleasures, desires,
and impulses,[8] all that is physical, sensual, sexual. This includes
everything we see, hear, touch, think about, and hunger for. Paul
took pains to list for us the works of the flesh in Galatians 5,
among them, immorality, impurity, sensuality, drunkenness,
and carousing. Surely no child of God would want to live a life
marked by these deeds! But only the Spirit's self-control can help
us avoid them.

Why? Because (as I've pointed out before) within every
believer a tremendous struggle goes on between the flesh and the
Spirit (Galatians 5:17). This "tug of war" between the flesh and
the Holy Spirit is a spiritual duel: The flesh and the Spirit "are
lined up in conflict, face to face."[9] So, to win the battle of self-
control, you and I have to recognize the conflict and rely totally
upon God's help and grace (Ephesians 6:10-13).

When Is Self-Control Needed?

As a fellow believer observed, "To a greater or lesser degree, if
you are alive you are tempted!"[10] Consequently, you and I need
God's self-control every minute of every day in every area of life

where we find ourselves facing temptation. We need the Spirit's help in the battle to resist fleshly urges in the common areas of life...like food and drink, purchasing and possessions, in all matters that are sensual and sexual in nature, and in self-indulgence of any kind.

Because self-control so often relates to the body (which is the temple of the Holy Spirit—1 Corinthians 6:19), we need to keep our bodies in subjection to the Lord. The reasoning goes like this:

> If the body is the temple, then the soul is the priest of the temple and should control the temple. Therefore, the soul should govern what the body does. When the body is tempted by the lust of the flesh, the lust of the eyes and the pride of life, the soul must say no! That is self-control. That body is disciplined by the soul to glorify God in all its actions.[11]

So, dear friend, we clearly need to be alert to our need for self-control in controlling our body. Then we'll be able to see the Spirit's grace of self-control in our lives.

What Does Self-Control Do?

When you and I are walking by the Spirit, His self-control is evident in our lives. That's when we'll reflect these strengths:

• Self-control controls and checks the self.

• Self-control restrains the self.

• Self-control disciplines and masters the self.

• Self-control holds in and commands the self.

• Self-control says, "NO!" to self.

A friend of mine wrote this list on a 3" x 5" card and taped it to the bathroom mirror to help her with a problem with overeating. I think her list is a great idea, and because it's applicable to a wide variety of problems, you may want to make such a list for yourself. You may also want to put the list in your prayer notebook. I know it always helps me to be reminded of God's pattern for self-control.

What Does Self-Control Not Do?

Looking at what God's self-control *isn't* also helps us understand this important fruit of the Spirit.

- Self-control does *not* yield to temptation.

- Self-control does *not* give in to desires.

- Self-control does *not* participate in sin.

- Self-control does *not* indulge itself.

- Self-control does *not* satisfy itself.

I warned you that self-control is a fruit of strength! By God's grace, we can be this strong—strong enough not to do these things.

What Is a Slogan for Self-Control?

In this final trio of spiritual fruit, faithfulness means—"*Do it!*" gentleness means— "*Take it!*" and now for our purpose of understanding, self-control means—"*Don't do it!*" In times of temptation we are to call on God for His strength, and then *don't do it!* In other words, don't give in to emotions, to cravings, to urges. Don't think or do what you know is against God's Word. Don't pamper yourself. Don't make the easy choices. Don't rationalize. And a thousand other "don't do its!"

As one pastor well explained, "The word *self-control* means 'the ability to say no.' It is an evidence of willpower that sometimes expresses itself in 'won't power.' It is the ability to say yes at the right time; yes to certain things, and no to others. It is that kind of inward strength that takes all the circumstances and experiences of life and subjects them to evaluation and then decides, 'This is right, this is in the will of God,' or, 'This is wrong, I will put it aside.' "[12] That is, don't do what you could—do what you should![13]

Learning from Others About Self-Control

As with the other fruit of the Spirit, God's Word comes to our rescue with vivid examples related to self-control. In fact, the Bible offers a gallery of people who did and did not possess self-control. I've selected a few of them.

David shows us self-control. Reading in 1 Samuel this week, I was impressed by King David's self-control. As we look for a moment at 1 Samuel 24, consider the events leading up to this point in David's life. After being anointed by the prophet Samuel to be king (16:13), David became the object of the jealousy and hatred of the reigning King Saul. And twice, when David played his harp for Saul, he had thrown his spear at David, hoping to kill him (18:11 and 19:10). Then, when David fled for his life, Saul and his soldiers ruthlessly pursued him.

Tired from the chase, Saul entered a cave, not knowing that David was hiding in the same cave (24:3). While David watched Saul from the shadows, David realized that he could—easily and for two good reasons—kill the king. After all, David had been anointed to be king. And, second, Saul was on an unjustified manhunt for David. There in the cave, it would have been easy for David to slay his adversary. Yet David won the battle for self-control. What did he do instead? He "persuaded his men...and did not allow them to rise up against Saul" (verse 7) and take his life. He told them, "Don't do it!"

David not only had the opportunity to kill Saul once—he had it twice! The second time, Saul, still in hot pursuit of David, lay sleeping at night in his camp, when David and a choice warrior entered the camp and stood over the king (1 Samuel 26:7). Concluding that God had delivered his enemy to him, David's companion begged, "Please let me strike him with the spear to the ground" (verse 8). In this case, David wouldn't even have to do the deed. Someone else would kill his enemy for him! Yet David restrained his friend, "Do not destroy him" (verse 9). Again, "Don't do it!"

David also shows us a lack of self-control. After Saul's death in battle, David finally reigned as king. But then a fateful chapter of his life begins with these words: "It happened in the spring, at the time when kings go out to battle, that David sent Joab and his servants with him and all Israel…but David stayed at Jerusalem" (2 Samuel 11:1). For whatever reason, David sent others in his place and remained at home in Jerusalem instead of going to war. Do you remember the portrait of "The Hero" from chapter 10? The hero was faithful: He was where he was supposed to be, and he was doing what he was supposed to be doing. Unfortunately, this statement was not true of David here, and this point marks the beginning of his great fall—as the next scene reveals.

One evening David took a stroll on his roof and, across the way, he saw a woman bathing by lamplight in the interior courtyard of her home[14]—*David saw.* Giving in to his desires, David next sent to find out who she was—*David considered.* As lust filled his thoughts and his heart, David gave in again and again and acted upon his fleshly desires until he sent messengers and took her and lay with her (verse 4)—*David acted.*

Do you see the progression of David's sin? At every step along the path of temptation, David gave in to his desires instead of exercising self-control and stopping the forward momentum of sin. He yielded to the sensual instead of choosing the spiritual. David could have chosen to stop and turn from evil at any stage along the way.[15] At any point, David could have said, "Don't do it!" But his failure to do this ensured his fall.

My friend, the situation is the same for you and me. With just one seemingly small wrong decision, just one failure to make the godly choice of obedience, just one moment when we let down, just one unchecked look or thought, even the strongest of the strong can topple into sin. This is why we must stay oh-so-near to God, keep a close check on our walk with Him, and cultivate the fruit of self-control with each thought, word, and deed. Praise God we can look to Him at any moment and receive His help and grace...and self-control.

Achan failed in self-control, too. When Joshua was the leader of God's people, the goods in the doomed city of Jericho were under a ban: Everything was to be burned and destroyed. But Achan acted unfaithfully in regard to the things under the ban (Joshua 7:1) and took some of the contraband. After a disastrous failure in a military raid, Joshua learned from God that someone had sinned against Him. With God's direction, Joshua confronted Achan. Hear Achan explain what happened: "When I *saw* among the spoil a beautiful mantle from Shinar and two hundred shekels and a bar of gold fifty shekels in weight, I *coveted* them and *took* them" (verse 21, emphasis added).

Does anything sound familiar here? Did you notice that this is basically the same pattern of fateful choices David made? And are you beginning to see the lessons we can learn from these men? Briefly stated, those lessons are: Don't stop, don't look, and don't listen. Don't do it!

Joseph and Potiphar's wife show us, respectively, self-control and the lack of self-control. Here's how it happened. The wife of Potiphar, an Egyptian officer of Pharoah and captain of the bodyguard

(Genesis 39:1), appears to have been living an empty life without purpose…until her husband purchased Joseph, the son of Jacob, to be his household slave.

And…evidently Joseph was extremely handsome (verse 6). Potiphar's wife looked with desire at Joseph and said "Lie with me" (verse 7). Suddenly Joseph had a choice to make. Choosing self-control, he successfully resisted her advance. Despite his refusal, Potiphar's wife spoke to Joseph day after day (verse 10), always extending the same invitation. And, day after day, Joseph had to again choose self-control. The day came, however, when no one was in the house but Potiphar's wife and Joseph. Filled with lust, desire, and passion, she grabbed Joseph. Again Joseph had to make a choice—and he chose to flee, leaving his outer garment behind in the woman's hand. Later this seductress used Joseph's cloak as evidence to imprison him for an act he did not commit.

This dramatic scene provides us with clear instruction on self-control. On the one hand, Potiphar's wife had no self-control. She allowed her thoughts and actions to be dictated by physical sensuality. *Looking* upon Joseph with lust…led to *thoughts* … that led to *actions* which were deeds of the flesh. In sharp contrast, Joseph shines as a positive example as he exercised self-control. He successfully resisted every opportunity to yield to temptation.

Why was Joseph able to stand strong? He explained the secret of his strength to Potiphar's wife: "How then could I do this great evil, and sin against *God?*" (verse 9, emphasis added). Joseph shows us the highest *motive* for self-control and the right perspective: He saw the incident from *God's* point of view and knew this act would be wrong. His *reasoning* was also right: He realized this deed would be a "sin against God." And Joseph's *focus* was also in the right place—not on himself, not on his desires, not on his flesh, but on God. What God wanted mattered more to Joseph than what he himself wanted.

Joseph models for us this truth: "The secret of discipline is motivation. When a man is sufficiently motivated, discipline will take care of itself."[16] As Jerry Bridges writes in *The Practice of Godliness,* "Ultimately, self-control is the exercise of inner strength under the direction of sound judgment that enables us to do, think, and say the things that are pleasing to God."[17] May that be our motive as we face the choices and temptations of life!

Struggling for Self-Control

As I was thinking about my own struggles for self-control, I listed the areas that challenge me most and cause me to turn to God for help. The first (and worst) for me is *food.* Life would certainly be easier if I didn't have to be around food. I know that God created our body to need fuel, but somehow the natural need and desire for food can so easily get out of hand. For instance, because I'm writing about food, my mouth and mind are suddenly yearning for something to eat—but it isn't time to eat. I don't *need* to eat because I just ate lunch. I just *want* to eat! So I'm forcing myself to sit here and keep my pen moving. I'm thinking, "Liz, just say no. Don't do it. Don't get up and go to the pantry. Fight it. You can have this victory with God's help. Stay seated and keep working."

Could I have something to eat? Of course. Would it hurt me to eat? Of course not—not now, anyway. But what would the blessings of not succumbing to the flesh be? For one thing, I'll continue my progress on this chapter. For another, I can have God's victory in this small thing. By saying no, I build a track record with Him and gain experience that will help me later when I face a large thing.

I also struggle with my *thoughts*—so much so that I've written an entire book on the subject. *Loving God with All Your Mind* [18] is about how to have victory over thoughts that are not true to God's Word. The book details how to win that battle by focusing on what the Bible *says* versus what our emotions and feelings lead us to *think*.

Money is another daily challenge for many, if not all, Christian women. The world comes right into our home and tempts us to spend. I had pretty much said, "Don't do it" to spending by eliminating shopping from my schedule...but almost every day some kind of catalog shows up in my mailbox, along with advertising flyers for all kinds of intriguing items! And I don't even have to send any money to get these things—my junk mail abounds with offers for free credit cards! Salespeople call me with appealing deals. (I would do better if I taped a sign on the phone that says, "Don't do it!") All these sales pitches create a real temptation to love the things in the world (1 John 2:15).

Closely related to the issue of money is the matter of *possessions*. I'm like every homemaker who loves having a nice home with all the little touches that make it a cozy and pleasant place— all the little touches that happen to cost money! When our family moved to Singapore for a term on the mission field, we sold or gave away almost everything we owned. But guess what? When we came back to the United States, I got to start all over again! Early every Saturday morning I left the house with $25 cash and went to garage sales. Quickly the day came when I had replaced everything—and added a few extras! At that point I came face-to-face with the fact that I was addicted to the thrill, the hunt, the anticipation I experienced as I drove up to each sale, salivating and tingling over the unknown. I had to start telling myself, "Don't do it" on Saturday mornings. I had to curb myself, hold myself back, and control my desires. Imagine this great struggle over what our Lord calls the "stuff in the house" (Luke 17:31 KJV)!

Last in the list of challenges I face is *coffee,* undoubtedly the most difficult bodily craving I—with God's help—have had to handle. I love the smell of coffee, the taste of coffee, and the buzz it gives. I love the warmth of coffee and the ritual of sitting down over a cup of coffee. But I reached the point when coffee was controlling my life! Coffee—not God—was my first waking thought. Coffee—not prayer—was my first waking need. Serving myself coffee—not serving my family—was my first concern each day. I got to the place where I couldn't think or function without coffee. I couldn't teach God's Word without it. I couldn't plan or write or work or drive without that warm cup in my hand. I knew I was in real trouble when I began the "drive thru" habit...not for hamburgers or french fries, but for coffee—and always a large!

The day finally came when I recognized that I had no self-control when it came to coffee. In fact, I was way out of control! Reluctantly I decided to curb my coffee drinking and bring it back under control. I had to choose to say, "Liz, don't do it" to some of my coffee.

Before you get the wrong idea, I want to say that everyone else I know seems to be able to drink coffee without any problems. Jim is one of those people. I fix him coffee every morning, but he's able to apply God's principle of moderation to his coffee intake. In all the areas I've shared—not just my coffee habit—you and I are to exercise discernment and wisdom as well as self-control.

Now your list of fleshly temptations probably looks different than mine. But the battle over each allurement is won in the same way, dear friend: by calling upon God and relying on the gift of His self-control; by asking Him for fresh strength to say, "Don't do it" one more time. Depending upon God's strength like this is the key to cultivating His self-control in our life.

Nurturing Self-Control

With its accounts of people who exhibited self-control and

those who didn't, the Bible teaches much about nurturing self-control. Maybe these instructions drawn from God's Word will help you begin cultivating that important fruit.

- Begin with Christ. Is He your Lord and Master? As one wise person has noted, "The beginning of self-mastery is to be mastered by Christ, to yield to his lordship."[19]

- Monitor your input. David's problem—and Achan's too—began with looking too long at the wrong things. Perhaps it was after his fall with Bathsheba that David wrote this advice: "I will set no wicked thing before mine eyes" (Psalm 101:3 KJV).

- Stay busy. Both David and Potiphar's wives failed because they had nothing to do. So make a schedule…and keep it! Volunteer to help others. Do whatever it takes to stay busy. By doing so, you will refuse to eat "the bread of idleness" (Proverbs 31:27), and you'll find yourself with less time to be tempted.

- Say, "No!" Solomon wrote, "Like a city that is broken into and without walls is a man who has no control over his spirit" (Proverbs 25:28). Echoing that truth is this thought: "The word *No* forms the armament and protective walls of the spiritual city.…Sometimes *No* can be a hard word to say, but it is the key to self-control, the word that the Lord blesses."[20]

- *Pray*. David "was a man committed to the reality of prayer. David prayed over nearly everything…except never once in the Bible do you find David praying about his love life. Not once.…It was perhaps the one area of his life he never yielded, and it almost crushed him."[21] So pray—about every aspect of your life!

God's good news for you and me, dear reader, is that we can claim His power, walk by His Spirit, exercise selfcontrol, and win the battle over fleshly temptation. Then we will wondrously display the beauty of Christ as we walk with Him through everyday life! What a wonderful God we have who makes the storehouse of His grace—His self-control—available to us!

13

Looking at Jesus' Applications

s you and I have been learning about the aspects of God's fruit of the Spirit and how to experience them in our life, Jesus has shown us much about what each of them looks like lived out by God's grace. I want us to look to Him again and seek to understand this final trio that deals with the discipline of self—faithfulness, gentleness, and self-control.

When we left chapter 9, Jesus had been forcefully apprehended and led away for His trial and crucifixion. How did He handle this series of events? And what was His mindset as He faced the cross? Peter, who watched these awful events unfold, can answer these questions for us. Although he strongly denied any association with Jesus when questioned by others (Matthew 26:69-75), Peter continued to follow his Master at a distance (verse 58). And with a few brief strokes of his pen, Peter summarizes our Lord's behavior so that we may follow in His steps:

> Christ...committed no sin,
> Nor was any deceit found in His mouth;

And while being reviled, He did not revile in
    return;
While suffering, He uttered no threats (1 Peter
2:22-23).

Jesus Committed No Sin

Peter's first comment is true about all of Jesus' life, not only
His final days. Throughout His earthly existence, Jesus committed no sin. You and I have probably experienced the momentary
reality of committing no sin when all is well and life is good. But
such favorable circumstances—a blessing from God—are times
when victory comes cheaply. But picture the worst of circumstances for a moment, the kind Jesus was experiencing, the kind
characterized by treachery, lying, false accusations, unjust punishment, brutality, physical abuse, fists, clubs, rods, whips, nails, and
a spear. Imagine committing no sin in this environment! Beloved,
that would unquestionably be the work of the Holy Spirit as He
enables us to walk through difficult situations without sinning!

But why was Jesus suffering so? Why was He being so harshly
mistreated? All His life He had...

Done well,
Done the right thing,
Done all that God asked and required of
    Him, and
Successfully carried out the Father's will for
    His life.
Jesus had...
    Taught God's truth,
    Healed God's creation,
    Fed God's people, and
    Taken light into darkness.
Jesus had also...

Preached the gospel to the poor,
Healed the brokenhearted,
Proclaimed release to the captives,
Restored the sight of the blind, and
Set free those who were downtrodden
  (Luke 4:18).

As Peter explains, Jesus suffered for doing what is right (1 Peter 2:21). The holy Son of God, He never in a single instance sinned. He lived His entire life without sin (Hebrews 4:15). Through the words of Peter and the writer to the Hebrews, God testifies to the complete sinlessness of Jesus. He, of all people, did not deserve to suffer in any way!

Even those who condemned Jesus knew He had committed no sin! Pilate told the chief priests and the multitudes, "I find no guilt in this man" (Luke 23:4). After Jesus returned from Herod's court, Pilate repeated to the chief priests and the rulers of the people, "Having examined [Jesus] before you, I have found no guilt in this man" (verse 14). Pilate explained further, "Nor has Herod, for he sent Him back to us; and behold, nothing deserving death has been done by Him" (verse 15). One final time Pilate asked the Jewish leaders, "Why, what evil has this man done? I have found in Him no guilt demanding death" (verse 22). No, our Jesus committed no crime. He committed no sin.

Do you realize that like our Lord and Savior who was consistently and completely victorious over sin, you and I can call upon God to help us make the right choices in life, choices which say *no* to sin? As believers, we should be primarily concerned about avoiding sin, not avoiding suffering. Scottish devotional writer Thomas Guthrie warned, "Never fear to suffer; but oh! fear to sin. If you must choose between them, prefer the greatest suffering to the smallest sin."[1] Can you make this the perspective of your heart, too?

Jesus Spoke No Sin

Jesus was not only sinless in deed. He was also sinless in word: "Nor was any deceit found in His mouth" (1 Peter 2:22). Even after careful scrutiny, Jesus' accusers failed to uncover any craftiness or trickery.[2] He had always spoken the truth. He had always spoken and acted with pure motives. Nothing of deceit or guile could be uncovered.

Furthermore, Jesus didn't talk back, but refused to answer at His trial. When falsely accused by the chief priests and elders, "He made no answer" (Matthew 27:12). When Pilate questioned Him, Jesus "did not answer him with regard to even a single charge" (verse 14). Caiaphas and the Sanhedrin challenged Him, too: "Do You make no answer? What is it that these men are testifying against You?" (Mark 14:60). Jesus' response? "He kept silent, and made no answer" (verse 61). Instead of pressing His case verbally to people who did not have ears to hear, Jesus silently submitted to harsh treatment and a cruel death which He did not deserve.

Jesus Did Not Resist

Jesus also did not resist His accusers and enemies. He refused to fight verbally or physically. We read, for instance, that while being reviled, He did not revile again (1 Peter 2:23). To be reviled means to be sharply bitten by words, to be subjected to harsh railing, to be cursed with a string of abusive words.[3] Such was the treatment our Jesus, the sinless Lamb of God, suffered! Put differently, "thus was the tender heart of the Lord Jesus wounded by totally depraved human nature."[4]

Just as Jesus didn't fight back when He was assaulted verbally, neither did He fight back when He was assaulted physically. Instead, "while suffering, He uttered no threats" (1 Peter 2:23). Here, "suffering" means being buffeted, struck with fists (Matthew 26:67). Peter is remembering the blows of the servants, the scorn of the high priest, the silent submission of Jesus, the stripes, the cross. The Greek language emphasizes that, "under sustained and repeated provocation, never once did [Jesus] break the silence. All the time during which He was the victim of abuse, He was not reviling back. All the time during which He was suffering, He was not resorting to threats."[5] One scholar points out that the words *suffered* and *threatened* have a progressive force in the original language, remarking that "even continuous suffering at the hands of the mob did not elicit from our Lord any retaliatory words."[6]

Of course sinful, retaliatory words wouldn't fit the picture of Jesus' perfect godliness! To react and respond is something you and I might do, but Jesus, when unfairly treated, did not utter threats, condemn His oppressors, or invoke judgment upon them. He kept His mouth closed. In the words of Isaiah, "He was oppressed and He was afflicted, yet He did not open His mouth; like a lamb that is led to slaughter, and like a sheep that is silent before its shearers, so He did not open His mouth" (Isaiah 53:7).

Oh, how precious is our Jesus! And how greatly my heart hurts as I think upon this scene of horror and evil. My Savior's response is sobering. It makes me think (and purpose!) that surely if He exhibited such graciousness—such faithfulness, and self-control—in these *evil* circumstances, I can do the same in my quieter sphere of life and service. Surely if He bore with tranquility the pain and suffering caused by His killers, I can quietly endure the ill treatment I receive from others. Surely if He kept His mouth shut when He was innocent, I can do the same, no matter what the false accusations and misunderstanding. But I also know that I can only do these things by the power of God's Spirit, who fills me with His faithfulness, gentleness, and self-control.

And now...a final prayer of thanksgiving...

It is with overflowing hearts, O Father,
That we whisper yet another "Thank You"—
This time for the grace of Your Son
    Who demonstrated complete faithfulness to You,
    Who accepted in gentleness such unjust
        mistreatment, and
    Who exhibited self-control in the harshest of
        circumstances
    As He walked to the cross to die for us.
May we receive Your grace…that we may
    Faithfully do all that You ask of us,
    Gently and quietly suffer all that comes our way, and,
    In control of ourselves, do nothing that
        dishonors Your worthy Name.
In Jesus' name, our Model and Savior and Lord. Amen.

EPILOGUE
Planning for Greater Growth

꧁꧂

Whew! We made it! You and I have completed our walking tour of the fruit of the Spirit! Together we strolled along the path, moving from group to group, from fruit to fruit. With God's Word as our guide, we read about each grace, each fruit—what each one is and how each can be cultivated as we walk with God.

I'm glad we were allowed as much time as we wanted with each fruit. We had time to study, time to enjoy, time to ask questions, time to discuss, and, most of all, time to appreciate. But now our tour is over; we've seen it all. We now know what it looks like to bear God's fruit in our lives.

As we leave these pages, we want to be sure to take God's message with us. It's one thing to talk about spiritual fruit, but God wants us—you and me—to live it out in our life. His Word describes for us what He wants our life to look like, what He wants others to see in us as we bear the fruit of His Spirit in real life.

God's Fruit Fleshed Out

But exactly how does the fruit of the Spirit flesh itself out in our life? I hope you can think of someone who exhibits the qualities of love, joy, peace, patience, kindness, goodness, faithfulness, gentleness, and self-control. I know I can, and his name is Sam Britten. Sam is an elder and a servant at our church, as well as director of the Center of Activities of the Physically Disabled at California State University at Northridge. Jim and I have known Sam for more than twenty years, but one of the students on campus helped us to appreciate him even more.

Judi had heard about the remarkable things going on in the center, which was just down the hall from one of her classes. So one afternoon, out of curiosity, she entered the room and stood silently watching. What she saw was Dr. Britten, down on his knees, helping and encouraging one of his disabled students. Hear what Judi—who wasn't a Christian, but who had heard of Jesus—said: "As I stood there watching Dr. Britten and saw his love and kindness and patience and gentleness with that student, I thought, 'This must be what Jesus was like!'" Daily, she was drawn to Dr. Britten's room, and again and again she saw this same scene. "Some days," Judi confessed, "I had to leave the room and go out into the hall so that I could weep. It was so moving to watch this man!"

Approaching Margie, one of Sam's assistants, Judi asked if she knew what made Sam like Jesus. Margie answered, "Oh, he's a Christian and he reads his Bible a lot and prays. In fact, we all pray together every day before the people arrive for treatment." Well, you guessed it. Soon Judi had bought herself a Bible. She began reading it and praying.

She also found a church, and within a year Judi had given her heart to Jesus.

God's Word Fleshed Out in You

Dear one, this picture of Sam Britten is what this book is all

about: Jesus in you and me; Jesus visible to others as we walk by
the Spirit; Jesus loving and serving others through us; Jesus on
display in us just as He is displayed in Sam Britten. When we
walk by the Spirit, we behave as Jesus did. And, as we've seen,
Jesus perfectly modeled each fruit of the Spirit. Filled with His
Holy Spirit, we, too, are to cultivate these graces so that we can
model Him to a needy world.

The apostle John wrote about this kind of Christlikeness in
1 John 3:2 saying, "When He appears, we shall be like Him."
Then, in the next verse, he tells us how we can become like Him
now: "Everyone who has this hope fixed on Him purifies himself, just as He is pure" (verse 3). And how does this purification
happen, and how can we help it happen?

> Everyone who truly believes that he will one day be
> like Christ...surely purifies himself and relentlessly
> pursues godliness as a number one priority. This is
> the mark of the true child of God. We are to feast
> our eyes upon Christ, upon as much of Christ as
> we can find in the sacred Scriptures. We are to do
> everything that we possibly can: We are to wrestle
> and fight and pray and be disciplined in order that
> more and more we become like Christ—whatever
> the cost—knowing that every sin that is overcome,
> every temptation that is resisted, every virtue that is
> gained is another step, another step, another step,
> another step towards that moment when we shall
> be like Him.

When Dr. John Blanchard, the wise speaker of these words,
finished this message, he prayed the following prayer: "We can
bless You for all of Your goodness *to* us, for the enabling of the
Holy Spirit *in* our lives, for every word of Scripture that has come
to burn in our hearts, for every step of progress that has been

made, for every victory that has been gained, for every temptation that has been resisted. And we can and do praise You as well,
knowing that it is only by Your grace and power that these things
were achieved."[1]

And now, my dear friend, may you and I make this prayer our
own as we continue to grow in our walk with God and cultivate
the fruit of His Spirit in our life.

Study Guide Questions

❧

The fruit of the Spirit is love, joy, peace, patience, kindness,
goodness, faithfulness, gentleness, [and] self-control.

GALATIANS 5:22-23

Chapter 1—Preparing for Greater Growth

God's Truth

- What is God's call to you in Galatians 5:16? What might
  happen in your life if you were to follow this instruction?

- According to Galatians 5:17, what conflict do believers
  live with? Give one or two specific examples of your struggle in this area.

- Review the "deeds of the flesh" listed in Galatians 5:19-21.
  Which deeds do you struggle with?

- Read Galatians 2:20, 5:24, and 6:14. What do you think
  these references to being "crucified" mean? How can the

truths of these verses change your view of daily life and, more specifically, your view of the struggles you identified in the two preceding questions?

• What is God saying to you in Galatians 5:24-25? What does the phrase "walk by the Spirit" mean? What does walking by the Spirit look like in your life?

My Response

• Read John 15:1-8. Abiding in Christ is another calling from God that enables us to bear His fruit in our life. What are some of the elements of fruit-bearing that result from abiding in Christ, according to these verses?

Verse 2—

Verse 4—

Verse 5—

Verse 8—

Chapter 2—Looking to God for Love

God's Truth

- Read 1 Corinthians 13:4-8a. Which aspect of love is most difficult for you to live out? Because fruit-bearing involves some effort on your part, what step will you take this week toward overcoming that difficulty?

- According to 1 John 4:7-8, who is the source of love? What do verses 20 and 21 of that chapter say about how we can know if someone loves God?

- What does Romans 5:5 teach about love?

- When do you find it hardest to love? As you answer this question, look at yourself as well as other people.

My Response

- What message did God have for you in the study of Ruth's love for her mother-in-law Naomi?

- Who in your life is hardest to love? As you think about that person, read Jesus' words in Luke 6:27-28. What specific instructions about the person you have in mind does Jesus give you here? What will you do this week to obey each of Jesus' commands? Don't forget to be specific!

- According to Luke 6:35, when you love the way Jesus tells you to love, what should you expect in return? And what can you ultimately expect?

- What can you do today to walk in love? Note at least one thing you will do today in each area.

  1. Remember the people at home (Titus 2:4)...

  2. Remember to look to the Lord (1 John 4:7)...

  3. Remember your assignment (Galatians 5:13)...

  4. Remember Jesus (Matthew 20:28)...

Chapter 3—Offering the Sacrifice of Joy

God's Truth

- What are believers commanded to do in 1 Thessalonians

5:16? According to Philippians 4:4, what is to be the source of a believer's constant joy? Explain.

- Read Psalm 32:3-4. How did unconfessed sin affect King David? Now look at verses 5 and 11. What did David experience once he confessed his sin? What area of sin might be interfering with your joy in the Lord? Take a few minutes to search your heart, confess your sin, and receive God's forgiveness.

- What perspective on suffering do you find in 1 Peter 1:6-8? And what reason for joy is given here?

- When do you find it hardest to experience joy in the Lord? How do circumstances generally affect your joy? What sacrifice of praise might you offer even when circumstances weigh you down?

My Response

- What message did God have for you in the study of Hannah's life and the circumstances that could have interfered with her joy? What can you do to follow her example on each of the following counts? Again, be specific.

  Quietly endure your pain

Release any thoughts of vengeance

Seek God in prayer

- As we discussed in the book, each fruit of the Spirit is commanded of you and me as God's children. Look now at the following scriptures and jot down your observations about these commands that affect your joy:

  Philippians 4:4—

  1 Thessalonians 5:16 and 18—

- How do these exhortations to rejoice and give thanks—no matter what—encourage you to offer the sacrifice of praise to God?

Chapter 4—Experiencing God's Peace

God's Truth

- Personal Peace—What instruction for peace does God offer you in Philippians 4:6a and John 14:1a? How do the truths of Romans 8:28 and 1 Corinthians 10:13 encourage you to rest in God's peace?

- What clues for how to know God's peace do you find in the story of Mary and Martha (Luke 10:38-42)? How can the four Scriptures you looked at (in the previous question) help you experience God's peace in that situation?

- Relational Peace—Read Colossians 3:12-15. What aspect of your life should the peace of God permeate? According to Romans 14:19, Hebrews 12:14, and 1 Peter 3:11b, how does this peace happen? What is your personal responsibility when it comes to ensuring peace in your relationships?

My Response

- Personal Peace—What concerns in your life tend to cause you anxiety and rob you of peace? More specifically, what current situation tempts you to worry?

- What sacrifice of trust will you make? And what aspects of God's character will you focus on?

- Relational Peace—What message does God have for you in Matthew 5:23-24? What steps will you take to make all of your relationships right? Again, be specific about the what and the when.

- As you look at your answers, what problems or issues are you prompted to bring to God right now so you can experience His peace?

Chapter 5—Looking at Jesus' Attitudes

God's Truth

- What do we know about the purpose of Jesus' life and death? See, for instance, Matthew 20:28.

- Read Matthew 26:36-46. Who witnessed Jesus' agony in the garden? According to Luke 22:45, how were the disciples handling their own distress at the time? What should they have been doing instead?

- What do Luke 22:44 and Hebrews 5:7 indicate about the intensity of Jesus' struggle in Gethsemane? According to Matthew 26:39, what was the determining factor in all that Jesus did and suffered?

- What spiritual attitude did Jesus exhibit as He faced the cross? See Hebrews 12:2.

- How do Jesus' words in Matthew 26:46 indicate that He knew God's peace?

My Response

- How do you normally handle difficult situations?

- What can you do at such times to be filled with God's love?

- What can you do in difficult situations to offer a sacrifice of praise? Think specifically about a challenge you currently face.

- In the situation you just referred to, what will you do to receive and know God's peace?

- What did Jesus do when He faced the overwhelming challenge of the cross? What will you do to make this the habit of your life?

- Take a minute to write out Matthew 20:28 on a card so that you can carry it with you and memorize it. Allow its truth to permeate your heart as you walk in the steps of Christ, your Savior!

Chapter 6—Resisting in Patience

God's Truth

- The Greek word for "patient" has been translated in at least three ways. Use a dictionary to define each term.

  Long-suffering

  Patient

  Tolerant

- Who in the Bible best models these characteristics of patience for you? How does that person encourage you?

- Read 1 Peter 2:18-23. When does patience find favor with God? What four natural behaviors did Jesus *not* exhibit when He suffered unjustly? What approach to suffering did Jesus choose instead?

- What current situation calls for you to have patience?

My Response

- Which person or situation in your life causes you the most pain, and why?

- Which definition of the three synonyms listed previously—long-suffering, patient, tolerant—is most meaningful to you in regards to this person or set of circumstances?

- According to Romans 12:19, why are we not to worry about or be involved in vengeance or retaliation against those who hurt us?

- Now consider Jesus' example (1 Peter 18:23). What attitudes and behaviors do you think God desires from you in your suffering? How can you achieve these attitudes and behaviors?

  By doing:

  By not doing:

- Here are a few useful tips for cultivating God's fruit of the Spirit patience in your everyday walk:

—Train yourself in long-suffering. How does Proverbs 19:11 challenge you?

—Lengthen your fuse. Read 1 Corinthians 13:4 and then make plans to lengthen your fuse! In what ways can you do this?

—Remove opportunities to sin. How can you follow God's advice found in Romans 13:14?

—Follow Jesus' example. According to 1 Peter 2:21, what can you do to follow in His steps?

—Pray. As Jesus showed in 1 Peter 2:23, prayer is one sure way to resist in patience. Why not pray now? And purpose to turn to God in prayer—as often as is necessary—every time you're in need of patience.

Chapter 7—Planning for Kindness

God's Truth

• Read the following references to God's kindness. Luke 6:35—To whom does God extend His kindness? Romans 2:4—What is the intention of God's goodness? Romans

11:22—What is the opposite of God's goodness? Ephesians 2:7 and Titus 3:4-5—What is the result of God's gentleness and kindness toward you?

• According to 2 Corinthians 6:6 and 2 Timothy 2:24, what qualities should characterize God's people?

• What commands does God give believers in Ephesians 4:32 and Colossians 3:12?

• Read 1 Corinthians 13:4. What does a failure to be gentle indicate?

My Response

• Who in your life tempts you to be unkind? What interactions with people especially challenge your efforts to be kind?

• Now choose one particular person who tends to bring out the opposite of kindness in you. Based on the discussion which closes the chapter, design a specific plan of action that will help you exhibit the fruit of kindness in your dealings with that person.

- Scripture tells us to show kindness to everyone. So take some time now to consider how you can make a deliberate effort to extend kindness to other people in your life. One habit I've cultivated is to take time each Sunday to make specific plans to show my care to others—family members, best friends, special people (such as those grieving a loss). I determine at least one act of kindness I'll do for each person during the week. This is truly planning to be kind—and it helps to cultivate a caring heart in me and hopefully blesses others.

  What about you? How will you plan to show some kindness this week? And who will your special target people be? Plan now for kindness and for caring.

Chapter 8—Giving in Goodness

God's Truth

- According to Matthew 5:45, what are some ways God practices goodness—and who benefits?

- What commands to Christians do you find in Galatians 6:9-10—and who is to benefit?

• What do the following verses say about goodness? Note those words addressed specifically to women.

Luke 6:27—

Ephesians 2:10—

1 Timothy 2:9-10—

1 Timothy 5:1—

Titus 2:5—

• What is God saying through these passages?

• Why do you need the help of the Holy Spirit in producing good works? See Romans 7:18-19.

My Response

• Displaying goodness is a matter of choice. That is, the manner in which you interact with and respond to others is up to you. And as a Christian, you're called to choose goodness.

—With that in mind, what negative behaviors have you exhibited in recent days or weeks that do not honor the Lord? What results came about because you refused to show goodness?

—With each negative behavior you mention, what would have been the proper response? And what positive results could you have enjoyed?

• As always, Jesus is our most wonderful example of goodness. As God in the flesh, He truly went about doing good (Acts 10:38). Read Luke 9:51-56. How did the disciples fail in goodness…and how did Jesus show them a better way? Is there a person in your life you would like to "call down fire" upon? What can you do to take upon yourself Jesus' gracious attitudes and actions and give in goodness instead?

• When it comes to goodness, be willing to take the initiative. Who do you know that needs your gift of goodness today? Your gift of God's love? Take the initiative and make the giving of goodness a priority. What a blessing we as God's women can be when we commit to advancing the happiness of others!

Chapter 9—Looking at Jesus' Actions

God's Truth

- In Matthew 26:47-68, who were the people or groups of people Jesus faced? List the different kinds of treatment He received from them.

- Now read Matthew 27:27-44. Add to your list of unkind people in Jesus' life and the unkind treatment He received from them.

- Did Jesus deserve the treatment He received? Was He guilty or innocent? Explain why you answered as you did.

- What could Jesus have done to defend Himself? What did He do instead?

- What do you learn from the way Jesus treated the man whose ear had been cut off? (see Luke 22:51).

My Response

- How do you usually respond to people who cause you pain?

- Exactly what can you do to resist in patience?

- What steps will you take to plan for kindness?

- What will you do to give in goodness?

- It seems that when we start moving down a certain path of "fleshly" conduct, things go from bad to worse. This was truly seen in Peter's actions the night of his denial of Jesus. What lessons can you take to heart from Peter's conduct on that most horrid of nights?

Chapter 10—Following Through in Faithfulness

God's Truth

- Define "faithfulness" in your own words.

- What do the following verses show you about faithfulness?

    Lamentations 3:22-23—

Romans 3:3—

Revelation 19:11—

Revelation 21:5; 22:6—

- In 1 Corinthians 4:2 and 1 Timothy 3:11, who is it that God is calling to be faithful? Why do you think God needed to call these individuals to faithfulness?

- In what circumstances do you especially need to hear God call you to greater faithfulness?

My Response

- Think back through your week. List any instances at home, in your relationships, or in ministry when you were unfaithful, when you proved unworthy of the confidence placed in you, when you didn't follow through on your commitments and responsibilities.

- What generally causes you to be unfaithful? What kept you from being faithful in the situations you listed previously?

- What does your unfaithfulness warn you about or indicate about your spiritual walk?

- List one action you can take to be more faithful in the areas where God has placed you.

  —As a Christian

  —As a wife

  —As a mother

  —As a daughter

  —As a home manager

  —As a worker

  —As a servant in the church

  —As a friend

  —As a neighbor

Chapter 11—Growing Strong Through Gentleness

God's Truth

- How does Jesus describe Himself in Matthew 11:29? What invitation does He issue His followers here? What effect has your acceptance or rejection of this invitation had on your life?

- What did Jesus say in Matthew 5:5 about those who are gentle? What do you think He means here? Make this question the focus of some study time if you're not sure.

- According to 1 Peter 3:4, how does God regard a gentle spirit?

- What does God command in the following verses?

  Galatians 6:1—

  Ephesians 4:2—

  Colossians 3:12—

  Timothy 6:11—

Timothy 2:24-25—

Titus 3:1-2—

• Why is gentleness so important to God?

• Why is gentleness so important to your walk with God?

My Response

• Gentleness is submissiveness to the will of God. In light of this definition, take a look at your life. In what, if any, areas of your life are you resisting God's will? What would help you bow before God in submission?

• What *thoughts* could help you cultivate gentleness in your life?

• What *actions* do you equate with gentleness?

• I'm sure by now you have taken the "giant first step" of identifying the greatest issue in your life. Now, consider how to apply the following principles to your problem as you walk in gentleness. For each principle, what do you need to do?

1. Accept—

2. Pray—

3. Refuse to complain or grumble—

4. Refuse to manipulate—

• Outline a plan for growing in the Christlike quality of gentleness.

Chapter 12—Winning the Battle of Self-Control

God's Truth

• Read 1 Corinthians 9:24-27. What does Paul describe here? What must be done to compete in the games (verse 25a)? According to Paul, what is his real opponent? What is Paul doing to control his opponent? What does this passage teach about self-control?

- Now read 1 Corinthians 7:1-9. What area of life is Paul addressing here? What does this passage teach about self-control?

- According to 1 John 2:16, what are three areas where we are especially vulnerable to temptation? What is the source of these areas of temptation? What source of strength for standing strong against these temptations does John identify here?

My Response

- These are the areas in which I'm most challenged when it comes to exercising self-control. In what ways do you struggle in these same areas?

  Thoughts—

  Money—

  Possessions—

  Addictions—

• In what additional areas do you struggle?

• What do the following guidelines from God's Word say to you regarding those areas of temptation you just identified?

Proverbs 4:14-15—

Proverbs 4:23—

Matthew 26:41—

1 Corinthians 10:31—

Colossians 3:16a—

• What ideas from "Nurturing Self-Control" will you put into practice today? (See pages 177-179.)

Chapter 13—Looking at Jesus' Applications

As we come to the end of our study about the fruit of the Spirit, we are blessed to look once again at the perfect life of our perfect Savior who perfectly lived out faithfulness, gentleness, and self-control. Let's pay close attention to the scriptures about Jesus Christ presented in this final chapter.

God's Truth

- Read 1 Peter 2:22-23. What does Peter tell you about Jesus here? Was He guilty of any sin?

- What does Hebrews 4:15 tell us about Jesus? How do you think He gained His victory over temptation? Explain how His victory over sin testifies to the presence of faithfulness, gentleness, and self-control in Jesus' life.

- Now read 1 Peter 2:19-20. What two kinds of suffering are contrasted in verse 20? Which kind of suffering finds favor with God? What is the right reason for you to suffer? And what does the issue of suffering have to do with the fruit of self-control?

My Response

- Evaluate the evidence of the following fruit in your life. Give a specific example or two of when you've seen the Spirit's grace gifts in your life and list areas which especially challenge you in each of these areas.

    Faithfulness—

Gentleness—

Self-control—

• What does Isaiah 53:7 tell you about Jesus? What does Jesus' example teach you here?

• What specific step can you take to live out God's grace and follow through in faithfulness?

• Also, what specific step can you take to live out God's grace and grow strong in gentleness?

• And what specific step can you take to live out God's grace and win the battle of self-control?

• In what ways do we see Jesus' faithfulness, gentleness, and self-control evident in the following passages?

    Luke 23:34—

    Luke 23:46—

- The next time you are faced with a situation that calls for faithfulness, gentleness, or self-control, what "action steps" can you apply from Jesus' example?

Epilogue

- I feel privileged to know Sam Britten, a godly man who exhibits love, joy, peace, patience, kindness, goodness, faithfulness, gentleness, and self-control. Who in your life fleshes out the fruit of God's Spirit? Give specific examples from that person's life—and thank God for his/her model.

- As we wrap up our study of the fruit of the Spirit, note what stands out from your reading, Bible study, and prayer.

  The most challenging biblical command

  The most encouraging truth from the Bible

  The most memorable word picture

  The most vivid Bible character

The most significant new insight into Jesus

The most important insight into yourself

• Now for our final question: How accurately are you presenting Jesus to a watching world?

• In closing, thank God for these lessons He has taught you...and ask Him to help you nurture these seeds He has planted by yielding to the work of the Holy Spirit so that His Spirit can continue to bring love, joy, peace, patience, kindness, goodness, faithfulness, gentleness, and self-control to full fruition in your life as you walk with Him.

Notes

Chapter 1—Preparing for Greater Growth

1. Merrill E. Unger, *Unger's Bible Dictionary* (Chicago: Moody Press, 1972), p. 382.
2. Alfred Martin, *John, Life Through Believing* (Chicago: Moody Bible Institute, 1981), p. 92.
3. Everett F. Harrison, *John, The Gospel of Faith* (Chicago: Moody Press, 1962), p. 91.
4. William Barclay, *The Gospel of John*, Vol. 2, rev. ed. (Philadelphia: The Westminster Press, 1975), p. 176.
5. Everett F. Harrison, *John, the Gospel of Faith*, p. 91.
6. Ibid.
7. H.D.M. Spence and Joseph S. Exell, eds., *The Pulpit Commentary*, Vol. 17 (Grand Rapids, MI: William B. Eerdmans Publishing Company, 1978), p. 295.
8. Albert M. Wells, Jr., ed., *Inspiring Quotations Contemporary & Classical* (Nashville: Thomas Nelson Publishers, 1988), p. 158.
9. John MacArthur, Jr., *Liberty in Christ* (Panorama City, CA: Word of Grace Communications, 1986), p. 92.
10. Phill McHugh and Greg Nelson, "Much Too High a Price." Copyright 1985 River Oaks Music Company/Careers–BMG Music Publishing/Greg Nelson Music. River Oaks Music Company Admin. by EMI Christian Music Publishing. All rights reserved. Reprinted by permission.
11. Henry Varley, *Moody Monthly*, June 1976, p. 97.

Chapter 2—Looking to God for Love

1. William Barclay, *The Letters to the Galatians and Ephesians*, rev. ed. (Philadelphia: The Westminster Press, 1976), p. 50.
2. H.D.M. Spence and Joseph S. Exell, eds., *The Pulpit Commentary*, Vol. 20 (Grand Rapids, MI: William B. Eerdmans Publishing Company, 1978), p. 293.
3. George Sweeting, *Love Is the Greatest* (Chicago: Moody Press, 1975), p. 20.
4. Edith Schaeffer, *What Is a Family?* (Old Tappan, NJ: Fleming H. Revell Company, 1975), p. 91.
5. Jerry Bridges, *The Practice of Godliness* (Colorado Springs: NavPress, 1987), p. 246.

6. William Barclay, *The Letters to the Galatians and Ephesians,* rev. ed., p. 50.

7. Mrs. Charles E. Cowman, *Streams in the Desert,* Vol. 1 (Grand Rapids, MI: Zondervan Publishing House, 1965), p. 97.

8. *The Amplified Bible* (Grand Rapids, MI: Zondervan Publishing House, 1970), p. 302.

9. John MacArthur, Jr., *Liberty in Christ* (Panorama City, CA: Word of Grace Communications, 1986), p. 88.

Chapter 3—Offering the Sacrifice of Joy

1. John MacArthur, Jr., *Liberty in Christ* (Panorama City, CA: Word of Grace Communications, 1986), p. 90.

2. William Barclay, *The Letters to the Galatians and Ephesians,* rev. ed. (Philadelphia: The Westminster Press, 1976), p. 50.

3. William Barclay, *The Letters of James and Peter,* rev. ed. (Philadelphia: The Westminster Press, 1976), p. 178.

4. H.D.M. Spence and Joseph S. Exell, eds., *The Pulpit Commentary,* Vol. 22 (Grand Rapids, MI: William B. Eerdmans Publishing Company, 1978), p. 6.

5. W.H. Griffith Thomas, *The Apostle Peter* (Grand Rapids, MI: Kregel Publications, 1984), p. 162.

6. John MacArthur, Jr., *The MacArthur New Testament Commentary, Galatians* (Chicago: Moody Press, 1987), p. 166.

7. A.A. Anderson, *New Century Bible Commentary, The Book of Psalms,* Vol. 1 (Grand Rapids, MI: William B. Eerdmans Publishing Company, 1972), p. 336.

8. Herbert Lockyer, *All the Promises of the Bible* (Grand Rapids, MI: Zondervan Publishing House, 1962), p. 10.

9. Margaret Clarkson, *Grace Grows Best in Winter* (Grand Rapids, MI: William B. Eerdmans Publishing Company, 1984), p. 21. Quoting from *St. Paul* by Frederick W.H. Myers, 1843–1901.

10. Charles Ray, *Mrs. C. H. Spurgeon* (Pasadena, TX: Pilgrim Publications, 1979), pp. 82-83.

11. *Life Application Bible* (Wheaton, IL: Tyndale House Publishers, Inc. and Youth for Christ/USA, 1988), p. 402.

12. John MacArthur, Jr., *The MacArthur New Testament Commentary, Galatians,* p. 166.

13. Jerry Bridges, *The Practice of Godliness* (Colorado Springs: NavPress, 1983), p. 134.

Chapter 4—Experiencing God's Peace

1. Kenneth S. Wuest, *Wuest's Word Studies in the Greek New Testament,* Vol. 1 (Grand Rapids, MI: William B. Eerdmans Publishing Company, 1973), p. 160.

2. William Barclay, *The Letters to the Galatians and Ephesians,* rev. ed. (Philadelphia: The Westminster Press, 1976), p. 50.

3. Howard F. Vos, *Galatians, A Call to Christian Liberty* (Chicago: Moody Press, 1971), p. 107.

4. Charles F. Pfeiffer and Everett R. Harrison, eds., *The Wycliffe Bible Commentary* (Chicago: Moody Press, 1973), p. 1297.

5. H.D.M. Spence and Joseph S. Exell, eds., *The Pulpit Commentary*, Vol. 20 (Grand Rapids, MI: William B. Eerdmans Publishing Company, 1978), p. 262.

6. Albert M. Wells, Jr., ed., *Inspiring Quotations Contemporary & Classical* (Nashville: Thomas Nelson Publishers, 1988), p. 152.

7. Curtis Vaughan, ed., *The New Testament from 26 Translations* (Grand Rapids, MI: Zondervan Publishing House, 1967), p. 265.

8. Ibid.

9. The shorter catechism of the Presbyterian *Book of Confessions*.

10. Gien Karssen, *Her Name Is Woman* (Colorado Springs: NavPress, 1975), p. 161.

Chapter 5—Looking at Jesus' Attitudes

1. John MacArthur, Jr., *The MacArthur New Testament Commentary, Matthew 24–28* (Chicago: Moody Press, 1989), p. 167.

2. Ibid., p. 166.

3. William Hendriksen, *New Testament Commentary, Matthew* (Grand Rapids, MI: Baker Book House, 1973), p. 916.

4. Ibid., p. 917.

5. Mrs. Charles E. Cowman, *Streams in the Desert* (Grand Rapids, MI: Zondervan Publishing House, 1965), p. 104.

Chapter 6—Resisting in Patience

1. Howard F. Vos, *Galatians, A Call to Christian Liberty* (Chicago: Moody Press, 1971), p. 108.

2. Kenneth S. Wuest, *Wuest's Word Studies in the Greek New Testament* (Grand Rapids, MI: William B. Eerdmans Publishing Company, 1973), p. 160.

3. Charles F. Pfeiffer and Everett F. Harrison, eds., *The Wycliffe Bible Commentary* (Chicago: Moody Press, 1962), p. 1297.

4. John MacArthur, Jr., *Liberty in Christ* (Panorama City, CA: Word of Grace Communications, 1986), p. 92.

5. Charles F. Pfeiffer and Everett F. Harrison, eds., *The Wycliffe Bible Commentary*, p. 1297.

6. William Barclay, *The Letters to the Galatians and Ephesians*, rev. ed. (Philadelphia: The Westminster Press, 1976), p. 50.

7. Alan Cole, *The Epistle of Paul to the Galatians, Tyndale New Testament Commentaries* (Grand Rapids, MI: William B. Eerdmans Publishing Company, 1965), p. 167.

8. John MacArthur, Jr., *The MacArthur New Testament Commentary, Galatians* (Chicago: Moody Press, 1987), p. 167.

9. Howard F. Vos, *Galatians, A Call to Christian Liberty*, p. 108.

10. Kenneth S. Wuest, *Wuest's Word Studies in the Greek New Testament*, p. 160.

11. Merrill F. Unger, *Unger's Bible Dictionary* (Chicago: Moody Press, 1972), p. 829.

12. George Sweeting, *Love Is the Greatest* (Chicago: Moody Press, 1974), p. 53.

13. John MacArthur, Jr., *Liberty in Christ*, p. 92.

14. H.D.M. Spence and Joseph S. Exell, eds., *The Pulpit Commentary*, Vol. 20 (Grand Rapids, MI: William B. Eerdmans Publishing Company, 1978), p. 287.

15. William Barclay, *The Letters to the Galatians and Ephesians*, rev. ed., p. 51.

16. Kenneth S. Wuest, *Wuest's Word Studies in the Greek New Testament*, p. 160.

17. Charles F. Pfeiffer and Everett F. Harrison, eds., *The Wycliffe Bible Commentary*, p. 1297.

18. William Barclay, *The Letters to the Galatians and Ephesians*, rev. ed., p. 51.

19. D.L. Moody, *Notes from My Bible and Thoughts from My Library* (Grand Rapids, MI: Baker Book House, 1979), p. 323.

20. William J. Peterson, *Martin Luther Had a Wife* (Wheaton, IL: Living Books, Tyndale House Publishers, Inc., 1983), p. 42.

21. William J. Peterson, *Martin Luther Had a Wife*, p. 62.

22. H.D.M. Spence and Joseph S. Exell, eds., *The Pulpit Commentary*, Vol. 20, p. 294.

23. William Hendriksen, *The New Testament Commentary, Colossians and Philemon* (Grand Rapids, MI: Baker Book House, 1964), p. 155.

24. Herbert Lockyer, *The Women of the Bible* (Grand Rapids, MI: Zondervan Publishing House, 1967), p. 158.

25. Herbert Lockyer, *The Women of the Bible*, p. 158.

26. Charles Caldwell Ryrie, *The Ryrie Study Bible* (Chicago: Moody Press, 1978), p. 420.

Chapter 7—Planning for Kindness

1. William Barclay, *The Letters to the Galatians and Ephesians*, rev. ed. (Philadelphia: The Westminster Press, 1976), p. 154.

2. William Barclay, *The Letters to the Galatians and Ephesians*, rev. ed., p. 158.

3. Ruth A. Tucker, *From Jerusalem to Irian Jaya* (Grand Rapids, MI: Zondervan Publishing House, Academie Books, 1983), p. 27.

4. John MacArthur, Jr., *Liberty in Christ* (Panorama City, CA: Word of Grace Communications, 1986), p. 93.

5. John MacArthur, Jr., *The MacArthur New Testament Commentary, Galatians* (Chicago: Moody Press, 1987), p. 168.

6. William Barclay, *The Letters to the Philippians, Colossians, and Philemon*, rev. ed. (Philadelphia: The Westminster Press, 1975), p. 157.

7. H.D.M. Spence and Joseph S. Exell, eds., *The Pulpit Commentary*, Vol. 20 (Grand Rapids, MI: William B. Eerdmans Publishing Company, 1978), p. 262.

8. John MacArthur, Jr., *The MacArthur New Testament Commentary, Colossians and Philemon* (Chicago: Moody Press, 1992), p. 155.

9. William Hendriksen, *New Testament Commentary, Matthew* (Grand Rapids, MI: Baker Book House, 1973), p. 505.

10. John M. Drescher, *Spirit Fruit* (Scottdale, PA: Herald Press, 1974), pp. 221-22.

11. John M. Drescher, *Spirit Fruit*, p. 210.

12. John M. Drescher, *Spirit Fruit*, p. 206.

13. Anne Ortlund, *Disciplines of the Beautiful Woman* (Waco, TX: Word, Incorporated, 1977), pp. 96, 98.

14. Alan Cole, *The Epistle of Paul to the Galatians, Tyndale New Testament Commentaries* (Grand Rapids, MI: William B. Eerdmans Publishing Company, 1965), p. 167.

15. C. Norman Bartlett, *The Gospel in Galatians* (Chicago: The Moody Bible Institute, 1964), p. 134.

Chapter 8—Giving in Goodness

1. John W. Cowart, *People Whose Faith Got Them into Trouble* (Downers Grove, IL: Inter-Varsity Press, 1990).

2. John W. Cowart, *People Whose Faith Got Them Into Trouble,* pp. 13-14.

3. Merrill F. Unger, *Unger's Bible Dictionary* (Chicago: Moody Press, 1972), p. 420.

4. Charles F. Pfeiffer and Everett F. Harrison, *The Wycliffe Bible Commentary* (Chicago: Moody Press, 1973), p. 1296.

5. Merrill F. Unger, *Unger's Bible Dictionary,* p. 420.

6. H.D.M. Spence and Joseph S. Exell, eds., *The Pulpit Commentary,* Vol. 20 (Grand Rapids, MI: William B. Eerdmans Publishing Company, 1978), p. 262.

7. W.E. Vine, *An Expository Dictionary of New Testament Words* (Old Tappan, NJ: Fleming H. Revell Company, 1966), p. 165.

8. John MacArthur, Jr., *The MacArthur New Testament Commentary, Galatians* (Chicago: Moody Press, 1987), p. 168.

9. H.D.M. Spence and Joseph S. Exell, eds., *The Pulpit Commentary,* Vol. 20, p. 262.

10. Kenneth S. Wuest, *Word Studies in the Greek New Testament,* Vol. 1 (Grand Rapids, MI: William B. Eerdmans Publishing Company, 1974), p. 160.

11. Howard F. Vos, *Galatians, A Call to Christian Liberty* (Chicago: Moody Press, 1973), p. 108.

12. Charles Caldwell Ryrie, *The Ryrie Study Bible* (Chicago: Moody Press, 1978), p. 1781.

13. Charles R. Swindoll, *Come Before Winter* (Portland, OR: Multnomah Press, 1985), p. 196.

14. William Barclay, *The Letters to the Corinthians,* rev. ed. (Philadelphia: The Westminster Press, 1975), p. 120.

15. William Hendriksen, *Exposition of the Pastoral Epistles, New Testament Commentary* (Grand Rapids, MI: Baker Book House, 1976), p. 365.

16. Ibid., p. 188.

17. Ibid., p. 107.

18. William Hendriksen, *Exposition of the Bible According to Luke, New Testament Commentary* (Grand Rapids, MI: Baker Book House, 1978), p. 558.

19. Oswald Chambers, *Studies in the Sermon on the Mount* (Fort Washington, PA: Christian Literature Crusade, 1960), p. 53.

20. Albert M. Wells, Jr., ed., *Inspiring Quotations Contemporary & Classical* (Nashville: Thomas Nelson Publishers, 1988), p. 82.

21. Neil S. Wilson, ed., *The Handbook of Bible Application* (Wheaton, IL: Tyndale House Publishers, Inc., 1992), p. 369.

22. Dan Baumann, *Extraordinary Living for Ordinary People* (Irvine, CA: Harvest House Publishers, 1978), pp. 83-84.

Chapter 9—Looking at Jesus' Actions

1. James Stalker, *The Life of Jesus Christ* (Old Tappan, NJ: Fleming H. Revell Company, 1949), p. 120.

2. Ibid., p. 121.

3. John MacArthur, Jr., *The MacArthur New Testament Commentary, Matthew 24-28* (Chicago: Moody Press, 1989), p. 194.

4. Ibid., p. 183.

5. James Stalker, *The Trial and Death of Jesus Christ* (Grand Rapids, MI: Zondervan Publishing House, 1972), p. 13.

6. William Hendriksen, *Exposition of the Gospel According to Luke, New Testament Commentary* (Grand Rapids, MI: Baker Book House, 1978), p. 989.

Chapter 10—Following Through in Faithfulness

1. Albert M. Wells, Jr., ed., *Inspiring Quotations Contemporary & Classical* (Nashville: Thomas Nelson Publishers, 1988), p. 69.

2. H.D.M. Spence and Joseph S. Exell, eds., *The Pulpit Commentary,* Vol. 20 (Grand Rapids, MI: William B. Eerdmans Publishing Company, 1978), p. 287.

3. John MacArthur, Jr., *The MacArthur New Testament Commentary, Galatians* (Chicago: Moody Press, 1987), p. 169.

4. John MacArthur, Jr., *Liberty in Christ* (Panorama City, CA: Word of Grace Communities, 1986), p. 95.

5. William Barclay, *The Letters to the Galatians and Ephesians,* rev. ed. (Philadelphia: The Westminster Press, 1976), p. 51.

6. Alan Cole, *The Epistle of Paul to the Galatians, Tyndale New Testament Commentaries* (Grand Rapids, MI: William B. Eerdmans Publishing Company, 1976), p. 168.

7. William Hendriksen, *Exposition of Galatians, New Testament Commentary* (Grand Rapids, MI: Baker Book House, 1974), p. 225.

8. Charles Caldwell Ryrie, *The Ryrie Study Bible* (Chicago: Moody Press, 1978), p. 1777.

9. Richard Shelley Taylor, *The Disciplined Life* (Minneapolis, MN: Dimension Books, Bethany Fellowship, Inc., 1962), p. 37.

10. Vanita Hampton and Carol Plueddemann, eds., *World Shapers* (Wheaton, IL: Harold Shaw Publishers, 1991), p. 17.

11. Edith Schaeffer, *Common Sense Christian Living,* (Nashville: Thomas Nelson, 1983), pp. 88-89.

12. Herbert Lockyer, *The Women of the Bible* (Grand Rapids, MI: Zondervan Publishing House, 1967), p. 101.

13. Richard C. Halverson, "Perspective" newsletter, 10/26/77.

Chapter 11—Growing Strong Through Gentleness

1. John F. MacArthur, Jr., *Liberty in Christ* (Panorama City, CA: Word of Grace Communities, 1986), p. 95.

2. William Barclay, *The Letters to the Galatians and Ephesians,* rev. ed. (Philadelphia: The Westminster Press, 1976), p. 52.

3. Howard F. Vos, *Galatians, A Call to Christian Liberty* (Chicago: Moody Press, 1971), p. 108.

4. H.D.M. Spence and Joseph S. Exell, eds., *The Pulpit Commentary,* Vol. 20 (Grand Rapids, MI: William B. Eerdmans Publishing Company, 1978), p. 262.

5. William Hendriksen, *Exposition of the Gospel According to Matthew, New Testament Commentary* (Grand Rapids, MI: Baker Book House, 1975), pp. 271-72.

6. William Barclay, *The Letters to the Galatians and Ephesians,* rev. ed., p. 52.

7. *Webster's New Dictionary of Synonyms* (Springfield, MA: G. & C. Merriam Company, Publishers, 1973), p. 812.

8. Albert M. Wells, Jr., ed., *Inspiring Quotations Contemporary & Classical* (Nashville: Thomas Nelson Publishers, 1988), p. 91.

9. William Hendriksen, *Exposition of the Gospel According to Matthew,* p. 765.

10. Merrill F. Unger, *Unger's Bible Dictionary* (Chicago: Moody Press, 1972), p. 709.

11. Kenneth S. Wuest, *Wuest's Word Studies from the Greek New Testament,* Vol. 2 (Grand Rapids, MI: William B. Eerdmans Publishing Company, 1974), p. 78.

12. Alan M. Stibbs, *The First Epistle General of Peter, The Tyndale New Testament Commentaries* (Grand Rapids, MI: William B. Eerdmans Publishing Company, 1976), p. 125.

13. Robert Jamieson, A.R. Fausset, and David Brown, *Commentary on the Whole Bible* (Grand Rapids, MI: Zondervan Publishing House, 1973), p. 14-75.

14. Kenneth S. Wuest, *Wuest's Word Studies from the Greek New Testament,* Vol. 2, p. 81.

15. Albert M. Wells, Jr., ed., *Inspiring Quotations Contemporary & Classical,* p. 92.

16. W.E. Vine, *An Expository Dictionary of New Testament Words* (Old Tappan, NJ: Fleming H. Revell Company, 1966), pp. 55-56.

17. W.E. Vine, *An Expository Dictionary of New Testament Words,* p. 56.

18. Derek Kidner, *The Proverbs* (London: InterVarsity Press, 1973), p. 63.

19. Derek Kidner, *Psalms 1–72* (Downers Grove, IL: InterVarsity Press, 1973), p. 176.

20. Charles Caldwell Ryrie, *The Ryrie Study Bible* (Chicago: Moody Press, 1978), p. 841.

21. Gien Karssen, *Her Name Is Woman* (Colorado Springs: NavPress, 1975), p. 132.

22. J. Vernon McGee, *Luke* (Pasadena, CA: Thru the Bible Books, 1986), p. 24.

23. Herbert Lockyer, *The Women of the Bible* (Grand Rapids, MI: Zondervan Publishing House, 1975), p. 105.

24. Gene A. Getz, *Moses, Moments of Glory...Feet of Clay* (Glendale, CA: Regal Books, 1976), p. 138.

25. Ibid., pp. 139-140.

26. Don Baker, *Pain's Hidden Purpose* (Portland, OR: Multnomah Press, 1984), pp. 86-89.

Chapter 12—Winning the Battle of Self-Control

1. J. Oswald Sanders, *Spiritual Leadership,* rev. ed. (Chicago: Moody Press, 1980), pp. 71-72.

2. Robert Jamieson, A.R. Fausset, and David Brown, *Commentary of the Whole Bible* (Grand Rapids, MI: Zondervan Publishing House, 1973), p. 1275.

3. William Barclay, *The Letters to the Galatians and Ephesians,* rev. ed. (Philadelphia: The Westminster Press, 1976), p. 52.

4. W.E. Vine, *An Expository Dictionary of New Testament Words* (Old Tappan, NJ: Fleming H. Revell Company, 1966), p. 114.

5. Charles F. Pfeiffer and Everett F. Harrison, *The Wycliffe Bible Commentary* (Chicago: Moody Press, 1973), p. 1297.

6. John MacArthur, Jr., *Liberty in Christ* (Panorama City, CA: Word of Grace Communities, 1986), p. 96.

7. H.D.M. Spence and Joseph S. Exell, eds., *The Pulpit Commentary,* Vol. 20 (Grand Rapids, MI: William B. Eerdmans Publishing Company, 1978), p. 287.

8. Kenneth S. Wuest, *Wuest's Word Studies from the Greek New Testament* (Grand Rapids, MI: William B. Eerdmans Publishing Company, 1974), p. 160.

9. Archibald Thomas Robertson, *Word Pictures in the New Testament,* Vol. IV, p. 311.

10. Bruce Wideman, *Presbyterian Journal,* July 30, 1975, p. 7.

11. Robert C. Gage, *Cultivating Spiritual Fruit* (Schaumburg, IL: Regular Baptist Press, 1986), p. 126.

12. Dan Baumann, *Extraordinary Living for Ordinary People* (Irvine, CA: Harvest House Publishers, 1978), pp. 118-19.

13. John H. Timmerman, *The Way of Christian Living* (Grand Rapids, MI: William B. Eerdmans Publishing Company, 1987), p. 146.

14. Charles R. Ryrie, *The Ryrie Study Bible* (Chicago: Moody Press, 1978), p. 476.

15. *Life Application Bible* (Wheaton, IL: Tyndale House Publishers, Inc. and Youth for Christ, 1988), p. 475.

16. Albert M. Wells, Jr., *Inspiring Quotes Contemporary & Classical* (Nashville: Thomas Nelson Publishers, 1988), p. 58.

17. Jerry Bridges, *The Practice of Godliness,* (Colorado Springs, CO: NavPress, 1987), p. 164.

18. Elizabeth George, *Loving God with All Your Mind* (Eugene, OR: Harvest House Publishers, 1994).

19. Jerry Bridges, *The Practice of Godliness,* quoting D.G. Kehl, p. 175.

20. John H. Timmerman, *The Way of Christian Living,* pp. 147-48.

21. Luis Palau, *Heart After God* (Portland, OR: Multnomah Press, 1978), p. 70.

Chapter 13—Looking at Jesus' Applications

1. D.L. Moody, *Notes from My Bible and Thoughts from My Library* (Grand Rapids, MI: Baker Book House, 1979), p. 362.

2. Kenneth S. Wuest, *Wuest's Word Studies from the Greek New Testament,* Vol. II (Grand Rapids, MI: William B. Eerdmans Publishing Company, 1973), p. 67.

3. Kenneth S. Wuest, *Wuest's Word Studies from the Greek New Testament*, Vol. II, pp. 67-68.
4. Ibid.
5. Alan M. Stibbs, *The First Epistle General of Peter, Tyndale New Testament Commentaries*, p. 118.
6. Kenneth S. Wuest, *Wuest's Word Studies from the Greek New Testament*, Vol. II, pp. 67-68.

Epilogue—Planning for Greater Growth

1. John Blanchard, "The Most Amazing Statement in Scripture" (Grace to You, P.O. Box 4000, Panorama City, CA 91412).

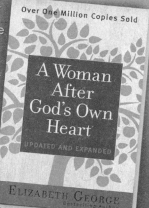
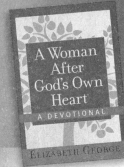

Raising a Daughter After God's Own Heart

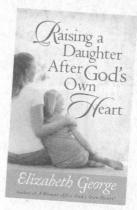

"The rewards of passing on the truths about God to your daughter will be great, and the fruit will last for all eternity."

—Elizabeth George

Help Your Daughter Become the Woman God Wants Her to Be

Your daughter has only one mother—you! God specially chose you for that role—to love her, equip her for life, and raise her up as a daughter after God's own heart. That means living as an example your daughter can imitate. How can you give your very best to your daughter and encourage her to love and follow God?

In *Raising a Daughter After God's Own Heart*, Elizabeth George—who raised two daughters—draws truth and guidance from Scripture, the wisdom of other moms, and personal experience. She also focuses on the fun and joy your special bond with your girl produces as you seek God's heart together.

Discover the ways in which you are a…

- cheerleader
- coach
- homebuilder
- marathon runner
- prayer warrior
- shepherd
- social secretary
- teacher

No one can fill these roles for your daughter better than you. And God has promised He will help you every step of the way!

For Your Daughters!

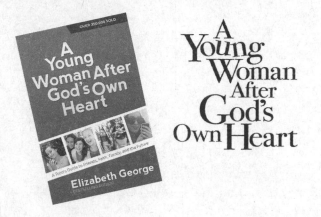

A Young Woman After God's Own Heart

What does it mean to pursue God's heart in your everyday life? It means understanding and following God's perfect plan for your friendships, your faith, your family relationships, and your future. Learn how to...

- grow close to God
- enjoy meaningful relationships
- make wise choices
- become spiritually strong
- build a better future
- fulfill the desires of your heart

As you read along, you'll find yourself caught up in the exciting adventure of a lifetime—that of becoming a woman after God's own heart!

Books by Elizabeth George

- Beautiful in God's Eyes
- Breaking the Worry Habit…Forever
- Finding God's Path Through Your Trials
- Following God with All Your Heart
- The Heart of a Woman Who Prays
- Life Management for Busy Women
- Loving God with All Your Mind
- Loving God with All Your Mind DVD and Workbook
- A Mom After God's Own Heart
- A Mom After God's Own Heart Devotional
- Moments of Grace for a Woman's Heart
- One-Minute Inspiration for Women
- Quiet Confidence for a Woman's Heart
- Raising a Daughter After God's Own Heart
- The Remarkable Women of the Bible
- Small Changes for a Better Life
- Walking With the Women of the Bible
- A Wife After God's Own Heart
- A Woman After God's Own Heart®
- A Woman After God's Own Heart® Deluxe Edition
- A Woman After God's Own Heart®— Daily Devotional
- A Woman's Daily Walk with God
- A Woman's Guide to Making Right Choices
- A Woman's High Calling
- A Woman's Walk with God
- A Woman Who Reflects the Heart of Jesus
- A Young Woman After God's Own Heart
- A Young Woman After God's Own Heart— A Devotional
- A Young Woman's Guide to Prayer
- A Young Woman's Guide to Making Right Choices

Study Guides

- Beautiful in God's Eyes Growth & Study Guide
- Finding God's Path Through Your Trials Growth & Study Guide
- Following God with All Your Heart Growth & Study Guide
- Life Management for Busy Women Growth & Study Guide
- Loving God with All Your Mind Growth & Study Guide
- Loving God with All Your Mind Interactive Workbook
- A Mom After God's Own Heart Growth & Study Guide
- The Remarkable Women of the Bible Growth & Study Guide
- Small Changes for a Better Life Growth & Study Guide
- A Wife After God's Own Heart Growth & Study Guide
- A Woman After God's Own Heart® Growth & Study Guide
- A Woman's Call to Prayer Growth & Study Guide
- A Woman's High Calling Growth & Study Guide
- A Woman Who Reflects the Heart of Jesus Growth & Study Guide

Children's Books

- A Girl After God's Own Heart
- A Girl After God's Own Heart Devotional
- A Girl's Guide to Making Really Good Choices
- God's Wisdom for Little Girls
- A Little Girl After God's Own Heart

Books by Jim George

- 10 Minutes to Knowing the Men and Women of the Bible
- The Bare Bones Bible® Handbook
- The Bare Bones Bible® for Teens
- A Boy After God's Own Heart
- A Boy's Guide to Making Really Good Choices
- A Husband After God's Own Heart
- Know Your Bible from A to Z
- A Leader After God's Own Heart
- A Man After God's Own Heart
- A Man After God's Own Heart Devotional
- The Man Who Makes a Difference
- One-Minute Insights for Men
- A Young Man After God's Own Heart
- A Young Man's Guide to Making Right Choices

Books by Jim & Elizabeth George

- A Couple After God's Own Heart
- A Couple After God's Own Heart Interactive Workbook
- God's Wisdom for Little Boys
- A Little Boy After God's Own Heart

To learn more about Harvest House books and
to read sample chapters, visit our website:

www.harvesthousepublishers.com

HARVEST HOUSE PUBLISHERS
EUGENE, OREGON

About the Author

Elizabeth George is a bestselling author and speaker whose passion is to teach the Bible in a way that changes women's lives. For information about Elizabeth's books or speaking ministry, to sign up for her mailings, or to share how God has used this book in your life, please contact Elizabeth at:

www.ElizabethGeorge.com